Myth and Mayhem

A Leftist Critique of Jordan Peterson

Myth and Mayhem

A Leftist Critique of Jordan Peterson

Ben Burgis
Conrad Hamilton
Matthew McManus
Marion Trejo

Winchester, UK
Washington, USA

JOHN HUNT PUBLISHING

First published by Zero Books, 2020
Zero Books is an imprint of John Hunt Publishing Ltd., No. 3 East St., Alresford,
Hampshire SO24 9EE, UK
office@jhpbooks.com
www.johnhuntpublishing.com
www.zero-books.net

For distributor details and how to order please visit the 'Ordering' section on our website.

ISBN: 978 1 78904 553 6
978 1 78904 554 3 (ebook)
Library of Congress Control Number: 2019956980

A CIP catalogue record for this book is available from the British Library.

Design: Stuart Davies

UK: Printed and bound by CPI Group (UK) Ltd, Croydon, CR0 4YY
US: Printed and bound by Thomson-Shore, 7300 West Joy Road, Dexter, MI 48130

We operate a distinctive and ethical publishing philosophy in
all areas of our business, from our global network of authors to
production and worldwide distribution.

Contents

Also by Ben Burgis

Give Them an Argument, Zero Books (ISBN: 978-1-78904-210-8)

Dedicated to our families

Acknowledgements

Many of the arguments presented in this book were presented in earlier form in multiple outlets. These include *Merion West, Jacobin, Quillette, Arc Digital, The Michael Brooks Show,* and other forums. The authors would like to thank these outlets for their ongoing support in promoting their work and the kindness and patience of the editors. We would also like to thank our families and friends for their generosity and warmth in reading over earlier drafts and offering no-nonsense criticism. Much gratitude to our frequent collaborators, including Dylan De Jong, David Hollands, Amir Massoumian, Borna Radnik, Erik Tate and others. Their passion for the topic always inspired us to make sure the book was the best it could be. Finally, thank you very much to Greg Tallion. He set up the website for this text and provided vital feedback and assistance throughout its writing. Solidarity.

Jordan Peterson as a Symptom of...What?
By Slavoj Žižek
The art of lying with truth

The wide popularity of Jordan Peterson is proof that the liberal-conservative 'silent majority' finally found its voice. His advantages over the previous anti-LGBT+ star Milo Yiannopoulos are obvious. Yiannopoulos was witty, fast-talking, full of jokes and sarcasms, and openly gay—he much resembled, in many features, a representative of the culture he was attacking. Peterson is his opposite: he combines common sense and (the appearance of) cold scientific argumentation with a bitter rage perceiving a threat to the liberal basics of our societies—his stance is that of, 'Enough is enough! I can't stand it anymore!'

The cracks in his advocacy of cold facts against politically-correct dogmas are easy to discern. His big image is that of a radical leftist conspiracy: after communism failed as an economic system and there was no revolution in the developed-West, Marxists, he claims, decided to move to the domain of culture and morality, marking the beginning of 'Postmodern neo-Marxism'. Its goal is to undermine the moral backbone of our societies and thus set in motion the final breakdown of our freedoms...But this kind of easy criticism avoids the difficult question: how could such a weird 'theory' find such a wide echo? A more complex approach is needed.

Jacques Lacan wrote that, *even if* what a jealous husband claims about his wife (that she sleeps around with other men) is all true, his jealousy is still a *pathological* phenomenon: the pathological element being the husband's need for jealousy as the only way to retain his dignity—identity, even. Along the same lines, one could say that *even if* most of the Nazi claims about the Jews were true (i.e. that they exploit Germans, they seduce German girls, etc.)—which they are not, of course!—their anti-

1

Semitism would still be (and was) a pathological phenomenon, because it repressed the true reason why the Nazis needed anti-Semitism: *to sustain their ideological position.* In the Nazi vision, with their society construed as an organic Whole of harmonious collaboration, an external intruder is needed to account for divisions and antagonisms.

The same holds for how, today, the anti-immigrant populists deal with the 'problem' of the refugees: they approach it in the atmosphere of fear, of the incoming struggle against the islamization of Europe, and they get caught in a series of obvious absurdities. For them, refugees who flee terror are equated with the terrorists they flee from, oblivious to the obvious fact that, while there may be among the refugees also terrorists, rapists, criminals etc., the vast majority are simply desperate people looking for a better life. Likewise, causes of problems immanent to today's global capitalism are projected onto an external intruder. Here, we find 'fake news', a term which cannot be reduced to a simple inexactitude: if they (partially, at least) correctly render (some of) the facts, they are all the more dangerously false or misleading. Thus, anti-immigrant racism and sexism is not dangerous when it simply lies—it is at its most dangerous when its Lie is presented in the form of a (partial) factual Truth.

The alt-right obsession with Cultural Marxism (Peterson's 'postmodern neo-Marxism') signals its rejection of the fact that the phenomena they criticize as effects of the Cultural Marxist plot (moral degradation, sexual promiscuity, consumerist hedonism, etc.), are actually the outcomes of the immanent dynamics of late capitalism itself. (In *The Cultural Contradictions of Capitalism* (1976), Daniel Bell describes how the unbounded drive of modern capitalism undermines the moral foundations of the original 'Protestant ethic' that ushered in capitalism itself. In a new afterword added in 1996, Bell offers a bracing perspective on contemporary Western society from the end of the Cold War to the rise—and fall!—of post-modernism, revealing the crucial cultural fault-lines we face as the twenty-first century (then) approached. The turn towards culture as a key component of capitalist reproduction, and, concomitant to it, the commodification of cultural life itself, is precisely what enables capital's expanded reproduction (think of today's explosion of art biennales: Venice, Kassel, etc.): although they habitually present themselves as a form of resistance towards global capitalism and its commodification of everything, they are, in their mode of organization, the ultimate form of art as a moment of capitalist self-reproduction.

The term 'Cultural Marxism' thus plays the same structural role as that of the 'Jewish plot' in anti-Semitism: it projects (or rather, *transposes*) the immanent antagonism of our socio-economic life onto an external cause: what the conservative alt-right deplores as the ethical disintegration of our lives (feminism, attacks on patriarchy, political correctness, etc.) must have an external cause—because it cannot, for them, emerge out of the antagonisms and tensions of our own societies.

Before we blame some foreign intruder for the troubles of our liberal societies, we should always bear in mind that the true shock of the twentieth century was the First World War—all horrors that followed, from Fascism to Stalinism, are rooted in it. This war was such a shock for two reasons: First, it exploded after over a half-century of continuous progress in Europe (no large-scale wars, rise of living-standard and human rights). There was no foreign agent fomenting it; it was a pure product of the immanent tensions of Europe. Second, it was a shock but not an unexpected one—for at least 2 decades prior to it, the prospect of war was a kind of public obsession. The catch was that precisely this incessant talk about it created the perception that it cannot really happen: if we talk enough about it, it cannot take place. This is why, when it exploded, it was such a surprise.

Unfortunately, the liberal-leftist reaction to anti-immigrant populism is often no better than the way it is treated by its opponents. Populism and PC (the left-liberal political correctness) practise the two complementary forms of lying which follow the classic distinction between *hysteria* and *obsessional neurosis*: an *hysteric* tells *the truth in the guise of a lie* (what it says is *literally* not true, but the lie expresses, in a false form, an authentic complaint), while what an *obsessional neurotic* claims is literally true, but it is a *truth which serves a lie*. Populists and PC-liberals resort to both strategies: First, as obsessional neurotics, they both resort to 'factual lies' when they serve what populists perceive as the higher Truth of their Cause. For instance, religious fundamentalists advocate 'lying for Jesus' in order to prevent the 'horrible crime of abortion': one is allowed to propagate false scientific 'truths' about the lives of foetuses and the medical dangers of abortion; or, in order to support breast-feeding, one is allowed to present as a scientific fact that abstention from breast-feeding causes breast-cancer, etc.

Today, common anti-immigrant populists shamelessly circulate non-verified stories about rapes and other crimes of the refugees in order to give credibility to their 'insight' that refugees pose a threat to our way of life. All too often, PC-liberals proceed in a similar way: they pass in silence over actual differences in the 'ways of life' between refugees and Europeans, since even mentioning them may be seen to promote Eurocentrism. Recall the Rotherham case in the UK where, 3 years ago, police downplayed the nationality of the perpetrators in case anything in the case could be interpreted as racist.

The opposite strategy — that of lying in the guise of truth — is also widely practised on both poles. If anti-immigrant populists not only propagate factual lies but also cunningly use bits of factual truth to add the aura of veracity to their racist lie, PC partisans also practise this 'lying with truth': in its fight against racism and sexism, it mostly quotes crucial facts, but it often gives them a wrong twist. The populist protest displaces onto the external enemy the authentic frustration and sense of loss, while the PC-liberals use its true points (detecting sexism and racism in language and so on) to reassert its moral superiority and thus prevent true social change.

And this is why Peterson's outbursts are so efficient, although (or, perhaps, *because*) he ignores the inner antagonisms and inconsistencies of the liberal project itself: the tension between liberals who are ready to condone racist and sexist jokes on account of the freedom of speech, and the PC regulators who want to censor them as an obstacle to the freedom and dignity of the victims of such jokes, is immanent to the liberal project and has nothing to do with an authentic Left. Peterson addresses what many of us somehow feel goes wrong in the PC universe of obsessive regulation: the problem with him does not reside in his lies, but in the partial truths that sustain his lies. If the Left is not able to address these limitations of its own project, it is fighting a lost battle.

A reply to my critics

Just a couple of remarks in reply to numerous critiques of my comment on Jordan Peterson. I see two levels in his work. First, there is his liberal analysis and critique of PC, LGBTQ+ issues etc., with regard to how they supposedly pose a danger to our freedoms. Although there are things I disagree with in it, I also see in it some worthwhile observations. My difference with him is that—while critical of many stances and political practices of PC, identity politics, or LGBTQ+ positions—I nonetheless see in them an often inadequate and distorted expression of very real and pressing problems. Claims about women's oppression cannot be dismissed simply by referring to interests in *Fifty Shades of Grey*, the story of a woman who enjoys being dominated (as one of my critics claims); and the suffering of transgender people is absolutely all too real. The way racist and sexist oppression works in a developed liberal society is much more refined (but no less efficient) than in its direct brutal form, and the most dangerous mistake is to attribute women's inferior social position to their own 'free' choice.

Second, I find Peterson's fixation on political correctness and other targets as the extreme outgrowth of 'cultural Marxism' (a bloc which, in its 'postmodern neo-Marxist' form, comprises the Frankfurt School, the 'French' poststructuralist deconstructionism, identity politics, gender and queer theories, etc.) to have numerous problems. He seems to imply this 'postmodern neo-Marxism' is the result of a deliberate shift in Marxist (or communist) strategy: after communism lost the economic battle with liberal capitalism (waiting in vain for the revolution to arrive in the developed Western world), its leaders, we are told, decided to move to the domain of cultural struggles (sexuality, feminism, racism, religion, etc), systematically undermining the cultural foundations and values of our freedoms. In the last decades, this new approach proved unexpectedly efficient: today, our societies are caught in a self-destructive circle of guilt, unable to defend their positive legacy.

I see no necessary link between this line of thought and liberalism. The notion of 'postmodern neo-Marxism' (or its more insidious form, 'cultural Marxism'), manipulated by some secret communist centre and aiming to destroy Western freedoms, is a pure alt-right conspiracy theory (and the fact that it can be mobilized as part of a 'liberal' defence of our freedoms says something about the immanent weaknesses of the liberal project). First, there is no unified field of 'cultural Marxism'—some of today's representatives of the Frankfurt School are among the most vicious denigrators of the 'French thought' (poststructuralism, deconstruction); and many 'cultural Marxists' are fiercely critical of identity politics, etc. Second, any positive reference to the Frankfurt School, or the 'French thought', was prohibited in socialist countries—where the authorities were much more open towards Anglo-Saxon analytic thought (as I remember from my own youth)—so to claim that both classic Marxism and its 'cultural' version were somehow controlled by the same central agent has to rely on the very suspicious notion of a hidden master who secretly pulls the strings. Finally, while I admit (and analyse in my books) the so-called 'totalitarian' excesses of political correctness and some transgender orientations which bear witness to a weird will to legalize, prohibit and regulate, I see in this tendency no trace of 'radical Left' but, on the contrary, a version of liberalism gone astray in its effort to protect and guarantee freedoms. Liberalism was always an inconsistent project ridden with antagonisms and tensions.

If I were to indulge in paranoiac speculations, I would be much more inclined to say that the politically-correct obsessive regulations (like the obligatory naming of different sexual identities, with legal measures if one violates them) are rather a left-liberal plot to destroy an authentic radical-Left movement— suffice it to recall the animosity against Bernie Sanders among some LGBTQ+ and feminist circles (who had no problems with big corporate bosses supporting them). The 'cultural' focus of PC-liberalism and MeToo is, to put it in a simplified way, a desperate attempt to avoid the confrontation with actual economic and political problems, i.e., to locate women's oppression and racism in its socio-economic context: the moment one mentions these problems, one is accused of vulgar 'class reductionism'. Walter Benn Michaels and others have written extensively on it, and in Europe, Robert Pfaller wrote books critical of this PC patronizing stance, and has now started a movement called 'adults for adults'. Liberals will have to take note that there is a growing radical-Left critique of political correctness, identity politics and MeToo.

A note on my debate with Peterson
I cannot but notice the irony of how Peterson and I, billed in

the publicity for our debate as the big opponents, are both marginalized by the official academic community. If I understand it correctly, I was supposed to defend, at this duel of the century, the left-liberal line against neoconservatives...really? Most of the attacks on me are now precisely from left-Liberals (Chomsky; the outcry against my critique of LGBTQ+ ideology; etc.), and I am sure that if the leading figures in this field were asked if I'm fit to stand for them, they would turn in their grave even if they are still alive. It is typical that many comments on the debate pointed out how Peterson's and my position are really not so distinct, which is literally true in the sense that, from their standpoint, they cannot see the difference between the two of us: I am as suspicious as Peterson. So as I saw it, the task of this debate was to at least clarify our differences.

Let me begin with a point on which Peterson and I seem to agree: problematizing the notion of happiness as the goal of our lives. What if, to have a chance of happiness, we should not posit it as our direct goal? What if happiness is necessarily a by-product? Yes, a human life of freedom and dignity does not consist just in searching for happiness (no matter how much we spiritualize it) or in the effort to actualize one's inner potentials—we have to find some meaningful Cause beyond the mere struggle for pleasurable survival. (One should introduce here the distinction, elaborated by Kierkegaard, between genius and apostle: a genius expresses its inner creativity while the apostle is a bearer of a transcendent message.) However, two qualifications should be added here.

First, since we live in a modern era *(ed. note: not to be confused with the post-modern cultural condition within it)*, we cannot simply refer to an unquestionable authority to confer a mission or task on us. Modernity means that yes, we should carry the burden, but the main burden is freedom itself—we are responsible for our burdens. Not only are we not allowed cheap excuses for not doing our duty, duty itself should not serve as an excuse or something to be exploited (say, when I know someone will be hurt if I do my duty, I should never say 'sorry, I have to do it, it's my duty'). So yes, we need a story which gives meaning to our life—but it remains *our* story: we are responsible for it; it emerges against the background of ultimate meaninglessness.

Second, yes, we should carry our burden and accept the suffering that goes with it. But a danger lurks here, that of a subtle reversal—don't fall in love with your suffering: *never presume that your suffering is in itself a proof of your ethical value, or your authenticity.* In psychoanalysis, the term for this is 'surplus-enjoyment': enjoyment generated by pain itself (that is, *renunciation of pleasure* can easily turn into *pleasure of renunciation* itself). For example, white left-Liberals love to denigrate one's own cultural background and blame 'eurocentrism' for our evils—but it is instantly clear how this self-denigration brings a profit of its own: through this renouncing of their Particular roots, multicultural liberals reserve for themselves the universal position, graciously soliciting others to assert their Particular identity. White multiculturalist liberals thus embody the lie of identity politics.

This brings me to my next critical point. What I sincerely don't get is Peterson's designation of the position he is most critical about (not as the usual 'cultural Marxists', but): 'postmodern neo-Marxists'. Nobody calls himself or herself that, so it's a critical term—but does it hold? Peterson seems to like to give precise references, he mentions books, etc., so I would like to know his precise references here. I think I know what he has in mind: the politically-correct multicultural, anti-Eurocentric, etc. mess. But, where are Marxists among them? Peterson seems to oppose 'postmodern neo-Marxism' to the Western Judeo-Christian legacy. I find this opposition weird.

First, post-modernism and Marxism are incompatible: the theory of post-modernism emerged as a critique of Marxism (in Lyotard and others). The ultimate post-modernists are today conservatives themselves *(editor's note: as extensively written-upon by our Matt McManus).* Once traditional authority loses its substantial power, it is not possible to return to it—all such returns are today a post-modern fake. Does Trump enact traditional values? No! His 'conservativism' is a post-modern performance, a gigantic ego trip. In this sense of obscenely playing with 'traditional values', of mixing references to them with open obscenities, Trump—not Obama—is the ultimate postmodern president. If we compare Donald Trump with Bernie Sanders, Trump is a post-modern politician at its purest, while Sanders is an old-fashioned moralist. Yes, when we make political decisions, we should carefully think about possible non-intended actual consequences which may turn out to be disastrous. But I would worry here about the Trump administration—it is now Trump who wages radical changes in the economy, international politics, etc. The very term 'postmodern neo-Marxism' reminds me of the typical totalitarian procedure of combining the two opposite trends into one figure of the enemy (like the 'Judeo-Bolshevik plot' in fascism).

Second, can one imagine anything more 'Western' than post-modernism or Marxism? But which Western tradition are we talking about? In Europe today, I think the greatest threats to that worth saving in a European tradition are precisely those populist 'defenders' of Europe, like Salvini in Italy or le Pen in France. (No wonder they are joining hands with Putin and Trump, whose shared goals are to ruin European unity.) As for me, that is why I am unabashedly Eurocentric—it always strikes me how the very leftist critique of Eurocentrism is formulated in terms which only have sense within the Western tradition.

Third, Peterson condemns historicist relativism, but a historical approach does not necessarily entail relativism. The easiest way to detect a historical break is when society accepts that something (which was hitherto a common practice) is simply not acceptable. There were times when slavery or torture were considered normal, now they are considered unacceptable (except for torture in the US in the last decade or so). And I see MeToo or LGBTQ+ as part of this same progress—which, of course, does not imply that we should *not* ruthlessly criticize eventual weird turns of these two movements, however. And, in the same way, modernity means you cannot directly refer to the authority of a tradition—if you do it, it's a comedy, an ego trip (if not something much worse, as in fundamentalism).

Another oft-repeated Peterson-motif is the idea that, according to the 'postmodern neo-Marxists', the capitalist West is characterized by 'tyrannical patriarchy' (with Peterson here triumphantly mocking this claim, enumerating cases of how hierarchy existed not only in non-Western societies—but also in nature!). Again, I sincerely don't know which 'neo-Marxists' claim that patriarchy is the result of the capitalist West. Marx says the exact contrary: in one of the most famous passages from The Communist Manifesto, he writes that it is precisely capitalism itself which tends to undermine all traditional patriarchal hierarchies. Furthermore, in 'Authority and Family', an early classic of the Frankfurt School (the origin of 'cultural Marxism'), Max Horkheimer is far from just condemning modern patriarchal family—he describes how the paternal role model can provide to a youngster a stable support to resist social pressure. As his colleague Adorno pointed out, totalitarian leaders like Hitler are not paternal figures. (And I am well aware of the obsession of post-colonial and feminist theorists with patriarchy, but I think this obsession is a reaction to their inability to confront the fact that the predominant type of subjectivity in the developed-West today is a hedonist subject whose ultimate goal in life is to realize its potentials and, as they say, re-invent itself again and again by changing its fluid identity.) What annoys me are theorists who present this type of subjectivity as something subversive of capitalist patriarchal order: I think such fluid subjectivity is the main fork of subjectivity in today's capitalism.

Let me now briefly deal with what became known as 'the "lobster" topic'. I am far from a simple social constructionism and I deeply appreciate evolutionary thought: of course we are [also] natural beings, and the fact that our DNA shares around 98 per cent with that of some apes means something—it sets some coordinates. Maybe I just focus on different authors, here: my references are Stephen Jay Gould, with his notion of ex-aptation (as opposed to adaptation), or Terrence Deacon with his notion of incomplete nature. Nature is not a completely determinist order; it is, in some sense, ontologically-incomplete, full of improvisations; it develops like French cuisine: is the origin of many of its famous dishes or drinks not, that, when they wanted to produce a standard piece of food or drink, something went wrong, and then they realized that this failure can be re-sold as success? They were making cheese in the usual way, but then the cheese got rotten and infected, smelling bad, and then they found this monstrosity (measured by the usual standards) charming in its own way; or, they were making wine in the usual way, when something went wrong with the fermentation, and so they began to produce champagne, and so on...

The same goes for tradition. Let me quote T.S. Eliot, the great conservative, who wrote, 'what happens when a new work of art is created is something that happens simultaneously to all the works of art which preceded it...the past should be altered by the present as much as the present is directed by the past. And the poet who is aware of this will be aware of great difficulties and responsibilities.' This holds not only for works of art but for the entire cultural tradition. Let's take the radical change enacted by Christianity (yes, I define myself as an atheist Christian). Does Christianity not break radically with the traditional order of hierarchy? It's not just that in spite of all our natural and cultural differences, the same divine spark dwells in everyone, but that this divine spark enables us to create the Holy Spirit, a community in which *hierarchic family values are abolished.* Democracy extends this logic to the political space: in spite of all differences in competence, the ultimate decision should stay with all of us—the wager of democracy being precisely that we should not give all power to 'competent' experts. It was communists in power who legitimized their rule by posing as (fake) experts. And something of the same order is implied by our judicial systems: a jury means that not only experts, but our peers, should be the ultimate judges. I mention these well-known facts only to point out how far they are from any hierarchy grounded in competences. And I, it is well known, am far from believing in ordinary people's wisdom: we often need a master-figure to push us out of our inertia and (I am not afraid to say this) force us to be free. Freedom and responsibility hurt, they require an effort. But the highest function of a true master is precisely to awaken us to our freedom.

So, what about grounding hierarchy in competence? Do men simply earn more because they are more competent? I think that social power and authority cannot be directly-grounded in competence: in our human universe, power (in the sense of exerting authority) is effectively something much more mysterious, even 'irrational'. Kierkegaard put this nicely when he wrote: if a child says he will obey his father because his father is competent and good, this is an affront to his father's authority—and Kierkegaard applies the same to Christ himself: Christ was justified by the fact of being God's son—not by his capacities (and every good student of theology can put it better than Christ). Here I simply claim that there is no such authority in nature: lobsters have hierarchy, but the top lobster among them has no *authority*; he rules by force, but he does not *exert power* in the human sense. Again, the wager of democracy is that power and competence or expertise should keep some minimal distance apart—this is why, already in Ancient Greece, popular vote was combined with lottery. In principle, capitalism abolishes traditional hierarchies and introduces personal freedom and equality; but are financial and power inequalities really grounded in different competences? (Liberal economist Thomas Piketty, in his *Capital in the Twenty-First Century*, provides an immense amount of data here...)

Another Peterson-motif is that, when an individual (or, presumably, a society) is in crisis, one has to offer it a mythic narrative, a story that enables it to organize its confused experience as a meaningful Whole. However, problems lurk here, too—Hitler was one of the greatest story-tellers of the twentieth century. In the 1920s, many Germans experienced their situation as a confused mess: they didn't understand what was happening to them, with military defeat, economic crisis and what they perceived as moral decay. Hitler provided a story, a plot (which was precisely that of the 'Jewish plot'): we are in this mess because of the Jews. And, incidentally, we should not forget here, that—as Freud already pointed out—the paranoiac construct is also a perverted attempt at healing, a story by means of which we try to organize our universe. We are telling ourselves stories about ourselves in order to acquire a meaningful experience of our existence. However, this is not enough. One of the most stupid wisdoms is: 'An enemy is someone whose story you have not heard.' There is, however, a clear limit to this procedure: is one now ready to affirm that Hitler was an enemy simply because his story was not heard?

Furthermore, ideological stories always locate our experiences into a social field. From what I know about Peterson's clinical practice, I fully appreciate what he's doing, his focus on bringing his patients to assume responsibility, self-reliance and purpose in life. But when he says: 'Put your house in order before you want to change the world,' my reaction is: OK, but why the choice? What if, in trying to achieve the first, you discover that your house is in disorder because of what is wrong in the world? Let's take Peterson himself: isn't he so active publicly (and in this sense trying to change the world) precisely because he realized how the predominant liberal ideology prevents individuals to put their houses in order? This is evidently true if you live in Congo or North Korea, but also with the extension of digital control in our world, etc. (In the old communist countries, those in power would love to see you focusing on putting your house in order—and leaving their power in the world undisturbed.)

The ultimate big story that guarantees meaning is, of course, religion. Is religion still the opium of the people? This, Marx's formula, needs to be seriously rethought today. Religion (that is, certain fundamentalist versions of it) is still an opium of the people. It is true that radical Islam is an exemplary case of religion as the opium of the people: a false confrontation with capitalist modernity which allows those Muslims to dwell in their ideological dream while their countries are ravaged by the effects of global capitalism—but exactly the same holds for Christian fundamentalism. Mike Pompeo recently said it is 'possible' that President Donald Trump was sent by God to save Israel from Iran: 'I am confident that the Lord is at work here,' he added. The danger of this stance is obvious: if you oppose US politics in the Middle East, you oppose the will of God...If and when God will judge Pompeo, we can guess what his defence will be: 'Forgive me, father, for I knew what I was doing!' – I knew I was acting on your will.

However, apart from 'neutral' expertise (the evocation of experts to justify choices which are clearly ideological), there are two other main opiums of the people at work today: opium and the people. When we think of opium, our first association may be evil Mexican cartels. But there will be cartels as long as there is big demand for drugs in the US and other developed countries. Maybe here also, then, before ridding the world from drug traffickers, we should put our house in order? Remember the horror of the two Opium Wars fought (not only) by the British empire against China: statistics show that, until 1820, China was the strongest economy in the world. From the late eighteenth century, the British were exporting enormous amounts of opium into China, turning millions of people there into addicts and causing great damage. The Chinese Emperor tried to prevent this, prohibiting the import of opium, and so the British (together with some other Western forces) intervened militarily. The result was catastrophic: China's economy decimated to half. But what should interest us is the legitimization of this brutal military intervention: free trade is the basis of civilization, therefore China's prohibition of opium import was a barbarian threat to civilization. Imagine such a similar act today: Mexico and Colombia acting to defend their drug cartels and declaring war on the US for behaving in a non-civilized way by preventing free opium trade.

But is schematic egalitarianism also not ideological? Yes—but is Marxism really egalitarian? Marx mostly mentions 'equality' only to make the point that it is an exclusively political notion, and, as a political value, that it is a distinctively bourgeois value. Far from being a value that can be used to thwart class oppression, Marx thinks the idea of equality is actually a vehicle for bourgeois class oppression, and something quite distinct from the communist goal of the abolition of classes. Marx even makes the standard argument that equal right 'can consist only in the application of an equal standard; but unequal individuals (and they would not be different individuals if they were not unequal) are measurable only by an equal standard insofar as they are brought under an equal point of view, are taken from one definite side only'.

So what about the balance between equality and hierarchy? Did we recently really move too much in the direction of equality? Is there, in today's US, really 'too much equality'? Does a simple overview of the situation not point exactly in the opposite direction? We recently learned that South Africa is the world's most unequal country—25 years of 'freedom' have failed to bridge the divide. Far from pushing us too far, the Left has gradually lost its ground for decades. Its trademarks — universal healthcare, free education, etc. — are continuously diminished. Look at Bernie Sanders' programme: it is just a version of what was, half a century ago in Europe, the predominant social democracy, but is today decried as a threat to the American way of life. Furthermore, I see no threat to free creativity in this programme — on the contrary, I see free healthcare and education etc. as absolutely essential to focusing one's life on more important creative issues (where, of course, we are not at all equal, where differences abound). Equality can also be a creating-of the space for as many as possible individuals to develop their potentials.

To conclude, allow me to just indicate how I see the fact (which bothered many 'Leftists') that the exchange between Peterson and myself was relatively peaceful and polite. The reason is not just that there are definitely aspects of his work which I appreciate (above all his clinical work, but also his critique of political correctness, his claim that white supremacism is identity politics appropriated by the Right, etc.). The basic difference between us was so evident that there was no need in that context to reassert it violently. And, ultimately, this difference is in our view of the present constellation of humanity: the way I see it, Peterson is much too optimistic — he thinks that capitalism will be able to manage its problems, while I think that we are approaching a global emergency-state, and that only a radical change can give us a chance.

To explore the importance of that difference without hyperbole is, I think, of renewed significance. Expressed with such symbolic efficiency, we find in this book a true violence impressing itself.

Jesus said, 'My kingdom is not of this world. If it were, my servants would fight to prevent my arrest by the Jewish leaders. But now my kingdom is from another place.'
'You are a king, then!' said Pilate.
Jesus answered, 'You say that I am a king. In fact, the reason I was born and came into the world is to testify to the truth. Everyone on the side of truth listens to me.'
'What is truth?' retorted Pilate.
John:18

Introduction

The first thing to note about Jordan Peterson is that he is a very smart man. The second thing to note is that many leftists refuse to acknowledge that. The 'Stupid Man's Smart Person' was how a November 2017 article in the Canadian magazine *Macleans* put it. And a lot of the other commentators aren't much kinder. Nathan J Robinson of the (great) socialist magazine *Current Affairs* made some great points in his critical article on Jordan Peterson, but just couldn't help but take some digs at weird sounding concepts like the 'Dragon of Chaos'. The *Jacobin* ran an ambiguously titled article called 'Jordan Peterson's Bullshit' in 2018 which accused him of 'pseudo-science, bad pop psychology, and deep irrationalism'. Of course these jabs at the man's intelligence pale next to some of the darker accusations. Perhaps the most famous was Pankaj Mishra's March 2018 essay 'Jordan Peterson and Fascist Mysticism' in the prestigious pages of the *New York Review of Books*. Mishra read *12 Rules for Life* as a hyper-masculinist text which disdained compassion and was built on fascist theoretical materials. Not to be outdone, the *New York Times* ran a really damning op ed in May 2018 calling him the 'custodian' of the patriarchy. And the list of damning accusations pile on and on, labelling Peterson everything from an Islamophobe to a racist.

We by no means wish to deny that some of these accusations have weight to them. Peterson's terminology and tendency to take himself very seriously set the man up for parody like few other public intellectuals. His willingness to say misogynistic and transphobic things, and support patriarchal institutions is damning. And he has shown more willingness than anyone should to appear with far-right iconography and figures, ranging from the white nationalist Lauren Southern to that modern swastika Pepe the Frog. All of this constitutes a serious swathe of points against him. But our intention in this book is to criticize Peterson the intellectual and professor at the University of Toronto, not to cast stones (however warranted).

The reason for such a project is there has been a notable lack of sustained left-wing efforts to actually engage with his ideas in a sustained manner. Once one looks past the public persona and into dense works like *Maps of Meaning* or the sustained psychological ruminations that make up *12 Rules for Life,* it becomes pretty clear that Peterson isn't just an unusually literate uncle saying controversial things at Thanksgiving dinner. He has some serious intellectual chops, and therefore needs to be taken seriously. In this book, we hope to do just that. Inspired by pioneering efforts like Marx and Engel's *The German Ideology* and more recently Corey Robin's *The Reactionary Mind,* we believe it is important for leftists to delve deep into the work of our opponents to demonstrate where they go wrong. And, perhaps more disturbingly, to acknowledge where they might have a few points worth listening to. And this is certainly the case with Peterson's work, which partly explains its popularity. While his account of so-called 'post-modern neo-Marxism' may be superficial and easily dismissed, there is something to Peterson's criticisms of left-wing activism and agitation. We ignore his salient points at our peril, since just carrying on as is can do little beyond shoring up support for reactionary parties.

This book will consist of three sections. Section One will be a monograph examining and criticizing Peterson's work as a whole, written by Matthew McManus. This section will consist of five chapters, running through everything from the intellectual roots of Peterson's thought to highlighting its failure to adequately address the great social problems of the age. It will also pinpoint where his critiques of leftist thought fall flat, while trying to provide a defence of certain positions where plausible. It will also highlight a few lessons for life we might take away from the Canadian professor. Section Two will consist of an extended analysis by Conrad Hamilton of Peterson's work on the Left. In particular, Hamilton criticizes Peterson for his skewed interpretation of much progressive thinking and theory. It concludes with a breakdown of the Žižek-Peterson Debate and what can be learned from it. Section Three consists of two essays by Marion Trejo and Ben Burgis. Each author will analyse a different element of Peterson's thought, offering a critical appraisal of its limitations when discussing feminist and logical points. Our hope is that these essays will round out this book and lay out a comprehensive set of critical observations about all aspects of his work.

Part I

Peterson, Classical Liberalism and Post-Modernism:
By Matthew McManus

Chapter One

Intellectual Roots

Peterson and the Inner Life

It might seem a little odd to include the biography of a still living figure into a critical book on him. But Peterson is no ordinary intellectual writing in a purely abstract matter about a topic related to their academic expertise. His major works all include substantial biographical components. These include a lengthy account of Peterson's intellectual and spiritual development in the Introduction to *Maps of Meaning*, ruminations of significant life experiences and relationships in *12 Rules for Life*, and even a somewhat pretentious letter written to his father at a young age which includes this modest observation:

> I don't know, Dad, but I think I have discovered something that no one else has any idea about, and I'm not sure I can do it justice. Its scope is so broad that I can see only parts of it clearly at one time, and it is exceedingly difficult to set down comprehensibly in writing...Anyways, I'm glad you and Mom are doing well.

On occasion these autobiographical elements are somewhat precious. But they do serve a more important purpose. Peterson is a psychologist working in a broadly existential philosophy. Needless to say, his work will inevitably have an intensely personal component to it, since his contentions are not simply about an objective subject matter. He is trying to demonstrate how to bring order to one's inner life by discovering meaning and authenticity in life. Like many of his intellectual forefathers — from Kierkegaard down to Jung — Peterson recognizes this as a task for each individual, including himself. And it must inevitably be explored through understanding one's self and psyche without deceit or obfuscation. Clearly Peterson did not excuse himself from these efforts, and it makes understanding his own inner journey helpful when trying to understand the intellectual outlook framing his work and ultimately politics.

Jordan Peterson grew up in the small town of Fairview in rural northern Alberta in 1962. For those unfamiliar with Canada, northern Alberta is considered unusually cold and isolated by the rest of us. He describes life in Fairview as relatively pleasant, with solidly middle-class and well-educated parents who provided security and encouragement from a young age. In *Maps of Meaning* he describes his family as nominally religious, with his mother being a true believer who attended church with the children and his father largely apathetic. Around the age of 12 he concluded that religion was for the 'ignorant, weak and superstitious' and left the church. He describes how virtually no one except his mother opposed this apostasy, and even she gradually became acclimated to Peterson's adolescent rebellion against the faith that had fostered him. Shortly before he went to university for political science, Peterson turned to mildly left-wing politics as a potentially new ideology to provide meaning in life. He participated in campus activism and joined the 'mildly' socialist New Democratic Party, associating with many young progressives. From very early on, though, Peterson recounts feeling out of place in the Left. He describes his colleagues as being unambitious and all too willing to blame society for their problems rather than assume personal responsibility for them. Peterson also found himself admiring the administrators and businessmen who ran the university, despite them technically supporting the inegalitarian structures his politics were opposed to. In both his major books, Peterson describes these tensions as coming to a head upon reading *The Road to Wigan Pier* by George Orwell. In the culminating section Orwell (who, it is worth noting, remained a lifelong socialist) painted a scathing picture of leftist intellectuals. He described them as feeling little connection to the poor they purported to help. Instead the basis of their politics was simply hating the rich.

Moreover, Peterson describes being largely bored and uninterested in the political science degree he was majoring in. Part of this seems to simply be the way the subject was taught at the University of Alberta, which he describes as economistic and largely oriented around social and institutional explanations of behaviour. Peterson regarded this as insufficiently foundational and become increasingly fixated on trying to solve bigger and more disturbing philosophical questions. Against the backdrop of the Cold War, he was concerned to discover why relatively affluent and technologically advanced societies would come so close to annihilating all human life on earth. This led him, perhaps inevitably, to the problem of good and evil. Peterson also decided to switch his intellectual focus to psychology. His early research topics involved travelling to high security prisons in Alberta to help his supervisor responsible for the psychological care of prisoners. This seemingly paradoxical interest in the darker underbelly of society persisted through his PhD work at McGill and post-doctoral research at Harvard, which focused on alcohol and drug abuse. In 1998 he was appointed a full professor at the University of Toronto, while also setting up a clinical practice. By most accounts Peterson was quite successful at both enterprises, becoming a well-regarded lecturer and highly cited academic while seeing about 20 clients a week. He also married his childhood sweetheart and fathered two children; the experience of raising them is frequently referenced in his books.

The tipping point in Peterson's life came in the mid-2010s. He had already flirted with becoming a more public figure, presenting a series of lectures on religion and self-help on YouTube which received a significant number of views. However, Peterson's big break came not because of psychology but because of politics. In September 2016 he posted a series of videos opposed to

Canada's *Bill C-16: An Act to Amend Canada's Human Rights Act and Criminal Code*. This Bill had been put forward by the Liberal government of Justin Trudeau, and would make it illegal for the federal government to discriminate against individuals on the basis of their gender expression. Peterson saw this as an attempt, alongside revisions to Ontario's Human Rights Code, to censor speech. He refused to comply with a demand that he address students by their preferred gender pronouns. During this time period, Peterson made a number of...questionable...claims about the potential legal ramifications of his stance. Despite chiming several times that he could be arrested for his position or lose his job, the University of Toronto sent two warning letters asking him to stop and then did nothing. Legal officials pointed out that the idea that Peterson would be subject to jail time was ludicrous, as nothing in *Bill C-16* or the Ontario Human Rights Code made it a crime to not use someone's preferred gender pronouns. Peterson also made some highly questionable claims about setting up an alternative post-secondary institution which would become accredited, which later turned out to be a dead-end project. The proposal's fantastic qualities certainly didn't discourage his new supporters from donating to Peterson on Patreon, and he quickly discovered a lucrative revenue stream which dwarfed his academic salary.

Despite these exaggerated claims about martyrdom, the conservative press in Canada and abroad lauded Peterson's position as a free speech warrior and anti-trans activist. He quickly shot to fame on the basis of the controversy, and other caustic remarks condemning left-wing thinking from Marxism to 'post-modern neo-Marxism'. Throughout 2017 and 2018 Peterson was largely successful in promoting himself as a centrist figure pushing against the radicalization of university campuses and politically-correct culture more generally. He won a truly embarrassing debate with Cathy Newman of Channel 4 News, pointing out blatant contradictions in her bad faith arguments against him. Throughout the year Peterson quickly became affiliated with other well-known critics of post-modernism and social justice, becoming a high-profile member of the so-called Intellectual Dark Web. He also initiated the worldwide *12 Rules for Life* tour, which saw Peterson touring the globe to mass audiences eager to hear him speak.

Things became a little rockier in late 2018 and 2019, after a number of embarrassing revelations. These included a picture of Peterson associating with far-right iconography like Pepe the Frog making the rounds, and an embarrassing lawsuit against Wilfred Laurier University where he alleged that faculty members had slandered him. Not a few commentators observed there was an irony in a free speech warrior trying to policy what other academics said about him through the law. More infamously, in early 2019 an image of Peterson appeared with a New Zealand fan on his *12 Rules for Life* tour. The image was a smiling Peterson next to man wearing blatantly Islamophobic clothing. The picture was taken shortly before a mass shooting in the country took the lives of dozens of Muslims. The whole affair allegedly cost Peterson a prestigious gig talking about the Biblical tradition at Cambridge. He produced an angry and often self-aggrandizing letter defending himself, but the damage was already done. Finally, in April 2019 Peterson engaged in a high-profile debate with the Slovenian leftist philosopher Slavoj Žižek, who is sometimes called the 'Elvis' of cultural theory. While the debate itself received a tepid reception overall (I quite enjoyed it), Peterson received a formidable amount of criticism for all but acknowledging he had very little first-hand knowledge of Marxist philosophy. He was also unable to give a clear answer when asked to describe who actually counted as a 'post-modern neo-Marxist', with Žižek rightly observing that most post-modern theorists were opposed to Marxism.

Despite these hiccups, Peterson remains perhaps the world's most prominent public intellectual. He has put both his clinical practice and teaching on hiatus, pretty much embracing his new-found celebrity. Many people love him, particularly those on the political Right. Some centrists and classical liberals are a bit more critical—particularly those with strong inclinations to empirical realism and atheism—but generally admire his stance against post-modernism and social justice activism. As mentioned in our introduction, Peterson is almost ubiquitously despised by the political Left. Some commentators like Youtubers Contrapoints and PhilosophyTube have been a bit more nuanced in their appraisal, offering highly critical but occasionally sympathetic evaluations of his work. But generally, he has been met with scorn, ridicule and protest by left-wing activists wherever he goes. Needless to say, this has done little to stymie his support amongst conservatives and centrists.

One of the things that becomes notable when looking at Peterson's biography is the sharp disjunction between his public persona and the greater depths seen in his written work and lectures. When reading *Maps of Meaning* or listening to a lecture on existential psychology, one is impressed by the care and depths of Peterson's thinking. Moreover, one cannot help but be moved by the passion shown towards his subject matter. It is easy to see how Peterson could become a beloved lecturer at the University of Toronto; he is anything but dry and scholarly. His writing and speeches pop with anecdote and life. And they also display an admirable willingness to look at all sides of the issue, and to delve into dark places few other academics dare to meander into. Contrast that with his public persona, which is aloof, arrogant and often even clownish. Hearing him posture as a martyr resisting the tyrannical interventions of the government of Canada, or basing a lecture on Marxism on a 40-page pamphlet written when Marx and Engels were in their 20s, is almost as compulsively eye rolling as endless editorials highlighting how many copies of *12 Rules for Life* have been sold. To understand how these contradictions emerge, we need to step away from Peterson's biography and into the murky realm of his intellectual work.

Man's Search for Meaning

I discovered that beliefs make the world, in a very real way — that beliefs are the world, in a more than metaphysical sense. This discovery has not turned me into a moral relativist however. I have become convinced that the world — that is — belief is orderly; that there are universal moral absolutes (although these are structured such that a diverse range of human opinions remains both possible and beneficial). I believe that individuals and societies who flout these absolutes — in ignorance or in wilful opposition — are doomed to misery and eventual dissolution. I learned that the meanings of the most profound substrata of belief systems can be rendered explicitly comprehensible, even to the sceptical rational thinker — and that, so rendered, can be experienced as fascinating, profound and necessary. I learned why people wage war — why the desire to maintain, protect and expand the domain of belief motivates even the most incomprehensible acts of group-fostered oppression and cruelty — and what might be done to ameliorate this tendency, despite is universality. I learned, finally, that the terrible aspect of life might actually be a necessary precondition for the existence of life, and that it is possible to regard that precondition, in consequence, as comprehensible and acceptable.

Maps of Meaning, Preface: *Descensus and Inferos*

At the opening of *Maps of Meaning* comes a quote from the Gospel of Matthew: 'I will utter things which have been kept secret from the foundations of the world.' Flash forward a few pages and one reaches the above quote in the Preface, which, to give a short list, promises that Peterson has discovered the answer to some modestly big questions. These include the nature of the world as a construction of beliefs in a 'more than metaphysical sense', the discovery that there are moral absolutes, the roots of social and political decay, how to understand the meaning of belief systems, why people wage wars and how to stop it, and how suffering relates to the meaning of life. While such theoretical sweep and audacity wouldn't be entirely out of place in the early nineteenth century, it's hard for a modern reader to swallow that any one person could provide answers to all these questions without a considerable amount of fudging. Saying that, it is hard not to admire the ambition and sweep of Peterson's interdisciplinary efforts. In some respects it represents the broadest effort to provide a relatively total explanation of individual and social beliefs and practices since the modernist heyday of Nietzsche, Freud and Hegel. It also constitutes the return of a certain form of idealism as a conservative force, necessitating the development of new kinds of materialist critiques. As we shall see Peterson argues that 'beliefs are the world in a more than metaphysical sense' (whatever that means, which is never clarified). In this respect he is endeavouring to move thinking back upside down to the Hegelian idealism so aptly criticized by Marx and Engels in *The German Ideology* and the *Theses on Feuerbach*. Defending leftism will in some sense mean turning thought upright again. More on that later.

So, what is it that Peterson actually believes and wants? In some respects, such a question can only be answered by turning to the problems any particular author chooses to engage with. And here I would contend that Peterson follows Nietzsche, Dostoevsky and Jung in being primarily concerned with the problem of nihilism. At its best, this is a quest for meaning in life. Consequently, his psychological work concerns how individuals can best adapt to the problem posed by nihilism in a variety of healthy and productive ways. Peterson's position becomes political when looking at how adaptations to nihilism become inadequate, resulting in dangerous social pathologies. These social pathologies lie at the root of all that is dangerous and vulgar in society. For instance, individuals may turn to the ideological comforts provided by totalitarian order as a solution to nihilism. Totalitarianism provides a total, but false and dehumanizing, ideology for interpreting the world. This can provide some comfort to individuals faced with choosing between the false God of Stalinism and life with no God at all. Or else individuals reject all belief systems as meaningless and false ideologies, and retreat into the cynicism and indifference characteristic of post-modernity. At points Peterson seems to suggest this cynical reaction is more characteristic of our times, though at others he seems more concerned that the rise of politically-correct campus activism constitutes a return to the totalitarian mindset. In either case, the individuals driven by nihilistic impulses are failing to deal with the problems in a healthy manner. This is where adopting 'rules for life' can be helpful as an antidote to chaos. These individual rules each have a specific purpose. But their overall intention is to help people find meaning in their lives, albeit without drastically changing the social or political conditions in which they live. Especially if they happen to be citizens of a liberal capitalist regime.

Now the problem of nihilism and the quest for some kind of transcendent—and it makes sense to use the word in its technical sense when talking about Peterson—meaning is a fine problem for any thinker. Indeed, there is a plausible philosophical case that it may well be the ultimate problem, though formulated in many different ways. For Nietzsche, the problem of nihilism might be posed in terms of 'life affirming values'. For the Martin Heidegger of *Introduction to Metaphysics* it may be the problem of Being: why is there something instead of nothing at all? For Derek Parfit the question may be 'what matters?' One might even frame the question in a somewhat different manner, by asking with Hannah Arendt and Theodor Adorno whether there can truly be life after Auschwitz? Do the evils of life and the world so trouble our conceits about human life having value that it would be better to drop them? Can we even talk about good or evil if human beings are simply destined to be the 'wolf' of their fellows? These are deep if potentially insolvable questions, and there is a sense in which the Left has failed to take them seriously. When bringing up questions about whether meaning has existence, there are still some who will dismiss them as 'bourgeois' or 'white affluent liberal' concerns which are secondary to the goals of political activism. One look around the world suggests that isn't really accurate. Many people who have endured the most potent suffering and exploitation have turned to questions about meaning to find some answer to their problems. Often these are religious explanations, which explains why some leftists post-Marx may find the questions a troubling ideological distraction. But this is too dismissive, ignoring the desire many people have for a deep explanation about the world. Brushing aside the 'oceanic' feeling Freud castigated as a superstition, or trivializing the emotional desires met by religion as an 'opiate' for the masses can only lead leftists to ignore an important dimension of human life and experience. Peterson has a point there, and not taking it seriously will cede a lot of ground to religious reactionaries who at least offer some kind of solutions.

The issue we take therefore isn't with the problem of nihilism and the quest for meaning. Whether taken up politically or examined individually, these are important issues. Where criticism needs to come in is the way that Peterson frames both the problem of nihilism and the solution. In particular he is keen to suggest that these can only be dealt with at the individual level. This is exceptionally odd, demonstrating one of the serious limitations to his idealistic approach to the issue. Peterson focuses a great deal on how ours is a nihilistic age and diagnoses this a primary social pathology since at least the beginning of the twentieth century. This may well be true, but one finds very little explanation in any of his works concerning how this happened. Why is it that the formerly meaning saturated world of tradition and religion began to give way to a nihilistic impetus to either dominate the world or abandon it? If the homey Orthodox religion of Russian peasants was so attractive, why would millions reject it for the modernist ideology of Leninism and then Stalinism? If life in rural liberal democratic societies was relatively affluent and stable, why would so many people in Fairview Alberta abandon the church for the spiritual vacuum of our secular age? The answers to these questions are complex, and multi-faceted. Not coincidentally, Peterson focuses on just two. The rise of scientific rationalism, and the emergence of rationalistic individuals determined to remake society along the lines of the former ideology. This ideology and the individuals who espoused it help bring about the emergence of nihilistic (post) modernity.

It is worth noting here the particular way the problem of nihilism is framed, since it will be extremely useful when understanding the limitations of Peterson's approach later on. Like all good idealists, Peterson argues it is ultimately beliefs which determine human actions. All other factors are secondary. It is a belief system, in this case scientific rationalism, which generated a certain kind of individual. These were often well educated, and even compassionate people who felt a strong compulsion to eliminate earlier religious belief systems and traditions. By doing so, they could clear the air for the rise of utopian political projects which would seek to use reason and science to bring about a utopian society here on earth. This ignored the more ancient injunction that man is irrevocably fallen, and any effort to create the Kingdom of God in the mortal realm would only collapse under its own hubris. As we shall see, there is a connection between this disparagement of the great utopian thinkers of the nineteenth century and the emptiness of the contemporary era which produces the dreaded post-Modern neo-Marxist intellectuals of today. To understand this, we need to look into the roots of the problem in the epochal shift to modernity.

The Emptiness of Post-Modernity

One of the often-implicit themes of Peterson's work is his complex relationship to modernity. Perhaps not coincidentally, Peterson's autobiographical account plays out the process of modernization in microcosm: early inculcation into a safe and traditionalist religious community with a devout parent, exposure to secular ideas followed by spiritual and intellectual apostacy, and an existential crisis of meaning which was followed by a partial return to the faith of his youth. Given this, it is sometimes difficult to disentangle Peterson's own thoughts about modernization from his highly personal and sometimes implicit characterizations. None the less understanding this is crucial to grasping the more intellectualized dynamics of his work to be analysed later.

Before we begin it is also worth noting one more autobiographical point which is informative; both when analysing Peterson's relationship to modernity and his account of the political Left. Peterson consistently talks about his experiences growing up in a Cold War atmosphere. He describes how friends and family members drifted with little sense of moral or political responsibility, since they were convinced that nuclear annihilation was on both the figurative and probably literal horizon. What was the point in trying to live a meaningful life if it was all going to be eradicated in the atomic flame of a Soviet bombardment? These are of course very serious concerns, and there was indeed good reason to be highly worried about the potential destruction of all life on earth throughout the middle of the twentieth century. But the intensity and ongoing focus of these experiences—still referenced by Peterson in his lectures today—demonstrate his attraction to the apocalyptic and epochal. This can be highly admirable, but there are considerable dangers. These can include an occasionally manic tendency to approach most political disputes along the same apocalyptic lines, with new iterations of the Marxist enemy assuming the role of the neo-totalitarians. This becomes a serious weakness when examining Peterson's efforts to carefully analyse leftist doctrines and literature. Modernity is (thankfully) not characterized by the eternal recurrence of the same and reducing political phenomena down to archetypal struggles against the same enemy in a new mask is reductive.

In either case let us begin looking into the problem of modernity more deeply. Like his intellectual forebears—from Dostoevsky down to Jung and Northrop Frye—Peterson regards modernity as characterized by a fundamental shift towards secularism. Earlier societies were in many respects highly different than ours. They tended to view life not in terms of what the world was objectively, as a matter of scientific fact. Indeed, Peterson stresses that it has taken many centuries to train individuals to regard the world along these thoroughly modernist terms. Ancient cultures from Babylon to the early Christians would draw no clear distinction between what the world was in a factual sense and what it means morally and religiously. Put another way, the notion that there could be some clear divide between facts and morality would have been incomprehensible to pre-modern peoples. The way they expressed this very holistic outlook was similarly different, as one might expect. Rather than compiling collections of empirical data, or developing dry systematic philosophies, they developed myths and heroic stories that implicitly both described the world and presented the moral purpose human beings had within it. In this sense, there was also no radical separation between human beings and the objects they apprehended and interacted with, since both were united within the same moral universe established by the divine. As

Peterson puts it quite early into *Maps of Meaning*:

> Before the emergence of empirical methodology, which
> allowed for methodical separation of subject and object in
> description, the world-model contained abstracted inferences
> about the nature of existence, derived primarily from
> observations of human behavior. This means, in essence, that
> pre-experimental man observed 'morality' in his behavior
> and inferred (through the process described previously)
> the existence of a source or rationale for that morality in the
> universe itself. Of course this 'universe' is the experiential
> field-affect, imagination and all—and not the 'objective'
> world constructed by the post-empirical mind. This pre-
> scientific 'model of reality' primarily consisted of narrative
> representations of behavioral patterns (and of the contexts
> that surround them) and was concerned primarily with the
> motivational significance of events and processes.

The most powerful of these mythological 'narrative
representations' were of course the major world religions and
theosophies, which Peterson has studied with care but variable
attention. These faiths inspired and gained tremendous power
because they codified—in language, symbol, musical expression
and a host of other mediums—a unified conception of what
nature was and our role within it. Because these codifications
adequately accounted for all these deep emotional and archetypal
needs within the human psyche, they became archetypal
narratives. To this day these remain so ingrained within our
collective unconscious, that almost any person could express
their idealized form without needing to be exposed to particular
examples. Someone who has never read the Bible will likely be
able to recognize the form of Jesus' passion story described in the
Gospels because she has encountered it a thousand times in the
watered-down forms of popular culture. An individual who has

never heard of Lao Tse would none the less probably understand the wise calls for orderly balance and self-control in the *Karate Kid*. These forms of symbolic codification were powerful enough that, as Peterson points out, we often remain beholden to their outlook without even recognizing it; a point Nietzsche continuously stressed in his writings about unwittingly secular forms of Christian morality.

From the standpoint of contemporary scientific materialism these religious myths seem naïve and even reactionary. But Peterson continuously stresses that they serviced an important emotional need, by providing many of us with a sense of the meaning of life. This was in turn conducive to generating a sense of moral responsibility in all, since each person had a strong belief that their life and actions mattered. Now Peterson acknowledges that this can be a terrifying sentiment, since many individuals are unable to bear the sense that each act they commit is being weighed and measured. It can also be conducive to many of the vices characteristic of the world's great religions, ranging from dogmatic suspicion to religious fundamentalism. But he also stresses that this is in many ways preferable to what occurs in the absence of a shared codified mythos.

With the advent of modernity, a crisis emerged. He observes in his lecture series on *Maps of Meaning* that, while there were important antecedents to the scientific method which preceded its revolutionary emergence over the past few centuries—the Greeks and Aristotle in particular being good examples— real science has only appeared on the scene quite recently. As a methodology, science offered an unprecedented means of assessing the now objective world from a factual perspective; indeed, Peterson sometimes suggests that the emergence of science was a precondition for thinking of the world factually. And of course, figures like Martin Heidegger in 'The Question Concerning Technology' would sympathize with such a position. But unlike the erstwhile Nazi sympathizer, Peterson is by no means anti-science. He praises the immense efforts and intellectual energies that went into developing a way of framing the world objectively. Moreover, it can certainly provide us with a great deal of guidance on how to interpret even highly ephemeral notions like consciousness of the personality in a more rigorous manner.

But Peterson also points out that science has proven such a powerful methodology, that it has in some places proven a destructive force. In particular science has an extremely difficult time apprehending the affective role that religious mythology plays in our lives. More generally, science finds it very difficult to ascribe meaning to the world. From a purely objective standpoint the world is simply as Wittgenstein described it in the *Tractatus Logico Philosophicus;* there are simply facts we can talk about referring to empirical objects and processes, and any meaning that might exist is resigned to the 'mystical' or dismissed as irrelevant to our understanding. Peterson consistently observes that as science has assumed ever greater status in Western societies, so too has its corrosive influence in destroying sources of meaning. How extensive that damage was only became really apparent in the nineteenth century, when existential writers in the vein of Nietzsche and Dostoevsky started to talk seriously about the 'death of God' at the hands of reason and what catastrophes this might provoke As is well known, their diagnostics were not pretty and Peterson frequently echoes the pessimism of his existentialist kin. What Max Weber called the 'desacralization' of the world was now well under way as we entered the twentieth century, though as we shall see later its root causes in capitalization go deeper than the very idealist account given in Peterson's work. Carl Jung, one of Peterson's most significant theoretical influences, articulates the position nicely in his late essay 'Approaching the Unconscious' which appears in the general introduction to his thought *Man and His Symbols*:

Modern man does not understand how much his 'rationalism' (which has destroyed his capacity to respond to numinous symbols and ideas) has put him at the mercy of the psychic 'underworld'. He has freed himself from superstition (or so he believes), but in the process he has lost his spiritual values to a positively dangerous degree. His moral and spiritual tradition has disintegrated, and he is now paying the price for this break up in worldwide disorientation and dissociation.

In particular, modernity and now post-modernity was and is characterized by the emergence of nihilism as a political and social phenomenon for the first time. Peterson acknowledges that there had of course been individual nihilists before, and his work gestures repeatedly to the work of Milton, Shakespeare and others for references on these points. But these individualized nihilists were rare and terrible figures, often striking awe and terror in their fellows. Figures like Macbeth possessed a kind of Satanic majesty in their time, being rare and frightening figures who blasphemed against the sacred order of God and nature codified in the religious mythology of the day. By contrast, Peterson observes that over the twentieth and twenty-first centuries nihilism has become a ubiquitous phenomenon. This is part of what others have called the 'dialectic of secularization' or, following Charles Taylor, we could call our entry into a secular age. What we have failed to recognize is the impact this has had on our outlook and behaviour, in part because the transition to a secular age has occurred so gradually and seemed part of a rationalizing process which simply strips the pre-scientific conceits of earlier peoples away. But the impact has been profound and far reaching according to Peterson. In many respects the movement towards nihilistic secularism has contributed to or perhaps even caused many of the great catastrophes of our time. These include the emergence of the totalitarian movements of the early and mid-twentieth century, and the growing cynicism and relativism of post-modern movements today.

Peterson's theoretical inspirations for this thesis on the correlation between growing secularism and the movement towards totalitarianism include Dostoevsky and Nietzsche. Both existentialists predicted that the death of God at the hands of his children would bring about a crisis in Western civilization. For Peterson, this crisis took the form of an intense movement towards secular ideologies which restored a sense of meaning to modern individuals set adrift in a Godless world. Such secular ideologies include intense fascistic nationalism on the political Right and the more universalistic creed of Marxist communism on the left. Interestingly enough, Peterson devotes very little time to actually exploring these ideologies in their historical specificity, preferring to deal with them at a high level of generality. Ultimately there is relatively little difference between fascism/Nazism and Soviet communism, since both ideologies wind up looking the same in practice. They subordinate the individual to the collective, insisting that the lives and liberty of the singular person are trivial next to the Mephisphophelean glory of the movement and its ideology. A society which is pathologically ill as a result of secularization can readily find such inhumane ideologies highly attractive, drawing the worst and most resentful individuals into the fold. The result is of course death and destruction on an epic scale, from the death camps of Auschwitz to the horrors of a Siberian prison camp.

Fortunately, the totalitarian movements and the ideologies associated with them appeared to have been completely defeated during the Second World War and the Cold War. Liberal individualism become ascendant (more on that later). But the social pathology generated by nihilistic secularism didn't disappear. We are still in the midst of the crisis of modernity. For Peterson nihilism has simply changed form. Rather than generating comprehensive and totalitarian ideologies, our nihilistic age is turning to more cynical and reductive creeds. Our insistence today is that we don't believe or care about anything, since there is nothing worth valuing. For Peterson, relativistic post-modern philosophies become highly attractive in such an environment. Like the totalitarian doctrines of old, Peterson believes post-modern philosophy insists that the individual is nothing and the group is everything. We are historically determined beings, no more responsible for our actions than we are capable of blaming others for their perceived sins. On the surface of it, post-modern nihilism takes the form of a kind of historical and political relativism with some surface appeals, given the emphasis on toleration and acceptance of a broad swathe of communities. But beneath these seemingly benign dispositions is a cynicism predicated on resentment at living in a meaningless world. Rather than trying to face up to the problems of nihilism, post-modern individuals wallow in resentment at being powerless and unable to value anything. This in turn leads them to attack anyone with the audacity to insist that life does have meaning, and they are wasting theirs. Like Dostoevsky's underground man, they tear down all individuals and doctrines which reveal their emptiness to them, often out of pure spite and malice. Often times this is couched in the rationalizing language of toleration, making the disposition all the more insidious and dangerous. What is required to counter this tendency is a recovery of meaning and moral responsibility. It is this impetus which underpins Peterson's seemingly banal calls to 'clean your room' and 'stand up straight with your shoulders back'.

The single most glaring weakness in Peterson's outlook is its relentless philosophical idealism, which often guts its explanatory power. It also accounts in part for the annoying tendency to lump complex and variable historical phenomena into tidy narratives where everything is determined by the same tensions in belief structures. Consider his account of modernity and the emergence of nihilistic secularism. Following figures like Heidegger, Nietzsche and others, Peterson largely blames the emergence of nihilism on the scientific revolution. Its division of the world into objective facts and highly specious values seemed innocuous enough in the time of Newton. But the cracks became a chasm by the time the nineteenth century rolled around, bringing about a titanic shift firstly to totalitarian ideologies and secondly to post-modern relativism.

Now there is of course some truth in this narrative. But Peterson's approach attributes an immense amount of causal significance to a belief in the scientific method, which belies the extraordinary complexity of secularization. Many more factors were at play, including material factors. The emergence of the liberal individualism so cherished by Peterson occurred in tandem with the scientific revolution, and its institutional and legal emphasis on freedom of inquiry and religion certainly played a role in eradicating the bases of faith. The spread of literacy made possible by the printing press—amongst the first books produced by Gutenberg was a copy of the Bible written in the lay language—allowed individuals to 'own' their faith and question it. And of course, the emergence of capitalism played an intense role in deepening and fostering secularism, as it removed traditionalist barriers to commodification. To give just one example, well stressed by Max Weber in *The Protestant Work Ethic and the Spirit of Capitalism,* the emphasis on profit gradually dissolved the communitarian religious ethos that underpinned society prior to the nineteenth century. Where once individuals saw themselves as part of a shared religious community, they increasingly saw themselves as competitors for work and resources. Compounding this was the economic impetus towards urbanization, which broke apart traditionalist rural communities by driving everyone to huge cosmopolitan cities. Over the course of barely a century, Western society went from being agricultural and rural—with social life often revolving around a church—to being urban and liberal. This was an epochal shift that cannot just be explained by claiming that 'beliefs make the world'. Marx and Engels seem to have captured the complexity of these dynamics far more accurately and vividly in *The Communist Manifesto*, where they talk about how liberal capitalism is profaning the world and that 'all that is solid melts in the air'.

Now our point here isn't to develop a counter-explanation for the emergence of secular nihilism and totalitarianism in Western societies; that would go well beyond the scope of this book. It is simply to point out that Peterson misses a great deal in his account, because he is so fixated on the idealistic belief that it is beliefs that make the world. This is not a politically neutral commitment either. It ties in integrally to Peterson's commitment to a conservative leaning liberal individualism. If the problem with contemporary society is purely the beliefs of its members, what one needs to do is morally insist that individuals change their belief systems and adopt another. If however the problem isn't just with individual belief systems, but with the material processes and institutions underpinning liberal capitalist societies then the problems become much bigger and the solutions would have to be more radical and transformational. But this is of course precisely what Peterson doesn't want, because he has a generally high opinion of liberal capitalist societies. So the problem must lie with the individuals who make up those societies, and of course their belief systems. The consequence of this is to raise issues up to such an idealized level that they can only be dealt with individually, and thus become depoliticized. So the Russian Revolution was in no substantial way prompted because individuals were angry at a distant monarchy which had brought them into a losing war and which couldn't feed its starving millions. The emergence of Nazism owed nothing to the faltering capitalism of the Great Depression or the institutional limitations of liberal politics, well mocked and manipulated by canny Nazis like the jurist Carl

Schmitt. Both are largely consequences of a loss of faith, and thus can only be dealt with internally rather than through political or economic reform. We will of course come back to this, since it explains a great deal about Peterson's continuous protestations against 'post-modern neo-Marxist' academics, and the strange tendency to present them as the greatest threat to freedom in the contemporary era (apparently self-described 'illiberal' right-wing populists like Victor Orban—currently ascendant across the globe—are a minor annoyance next to those damn Foucault scholars in social science departments).

Before we move into these more political concerns, it is important to grasp the deeper argument for this individualistic idealism. The roots of Peterson's thinking in the existential quest for meaning and the crisis of modernity become more significant when one sees how they are developed in his complex arguments about the self and its beliefs. These are primarily laid out in *Maps of Meaning*, his academic papers and of course the lectures which were his first major foray into the public sphere. We will take a look at how his philosophy is presented in these works before moving on to analysing his politics directly.

Chapter Two

The Generation of Meaning

The Structure of *Maps of Meaning*

Jordan Peterson's outlook is shaped by his personal interest in the question of meaning, and the broader social concern about the collapse of shared meaning under the pressures of scientific (post) modernity. However these factors cannot explain how the problem of meaning became a central one in the first place, whether for a young PhD candidate at McGill or for Nietzsche, Dostoevsky and the whole of Western civilization circa the nineteenth century. A more holistic approach is required that looks at the origins of human cognition and the way the problem of meaning evolved over the course of history, in particular to deal with the problem of suffering and eventually evil. This approach was spelled out at a theoretical level in *Maps of Meaning* in the 1990s, and despite updating his approach in various papers—in my opinion 'Religion, Sovereignty, Natural Rights, and the Constituent Elements of Experience' is the most important—and lectures, it remains his theoretical magnum opus thus far. The later *12 Rules for Life: An Antidote for Chaos* is an important book in spelling out its implications in far more concrete detail; particularly in clarifying how the disjunction between Order and Chaos is to be practically solved. But the later book is considerably less interesting in its intellectual innovations.

In a historical irony that might have amused the Marx of the *18th Brumaire*—'history always repeats itself, first as tragedy then as farce'—the structure of *Maps of Meaning* echoes that of a far earlier book by a prominent German idealist. I am speaking of course of Georg Hegel's *Phenomenology of Spirit*. And indeed, the parallels are perhaps not coincidental. Peterson has often

47

admitted his debt to the American pragmatists, who themselves were highly influenced by Hegelian thinking. And it would not be out of line to characterize Peterson's project as very much a right Hegelian effort at mediating the dialectical tensions of post-modernity through a restoration of the individual and traditionalism at the centre of politics. Before we get there though we must look deeper into the structure of Peterson's argument.

Like Hegel's *Phenomenology of Spirit,* the more recent *Maps of Meaning* has an onion like structure. It begins with an analysis of the universal individual largely stripped away of any meaningful historical relations with his fellows. The first two chapters of the book, 'Objects and Meaning' and the massive 'Maps of Meaning' generally run through how a singular human individual evolved over many centuries to cognize about the world she interacts with. These individuals tend to develop a normative sense that the world doesn't just exist as a collection of independent objects as modern scientific materialism might claim; indeed, this inclination runs counter to our natural way of apprehending reality as a realm of meaning. Initially at least, meaning for the single individual who has goals and projects they wish to accomplish in the world. These two chapters coincide nicely with Hegel's argument in *Phenomenology* about the passage of geist from apprehending the world as mere consciousness: through sense certainty, perception and finally as something which can be understood and manipulated through force.

Both Peterson and Hegel conclude that eventually, our early person moves from a myopic kind of individual consciousness to a richer 'shared map of the world' we form through our relations with other conscious humans. Peterson characterizes this in chapters three and four as the 'adoption of a shared map' which can be challenged or destabilized by anomaly. In these chapters, far less attention is paid directly to the individual psyche, and a lot more to the collectively developed mythological narratives which code the shared sense of meaning held by a community. They are perhaps the most Jungian in the book, consisting of long analyses of different mythological narratives. Peterson makes the challenging claim that many of these myths share a universal commitment articulated to the same values and beliefs, which are expressed through very different forms of symbolic coding. Looking past the surface to the shared meaning beneath is the task for the reflective psychoanalyst. In particular, Peterson contends that an archetypal division between Order and Chaos, which as far as I can see are the closest things to the 'more than metaphysical' forces discussed earlier, is expressed in shared narratives about the Great/Tyrannical father and the Great/Destructive mother. The father stands for order and the mother for chaos, both vital and necessary but both potentially destructive. These coincide with the central chapters of *Phenomenology* on the topic of the family, the state, organized religion and the vital but dangerous role they play both advancing and inhibiting freedom. Peterson as we will see has a similarly ambiguous view, though since the publication of *Maps of Meaning* he seems to come pretty clearly down on the side of 'order' as the subtitle of his second book *An Antidote to Chaos* suggests. The problem with these characterizations is that they do not adequately counter the primary threat to meaning in general, which is neither order or chaos but evil.

The last chapter of *Maps of Meaning* takes up this problem. The initial temptation to evil stems from the existence of 'the anomaly', which brings the spectre of death and destruction to the shared map of meaning as its material instantiations through the mere fact of its otherness. Healthy communities are able to deal with the presence of the anomalous without collapsing into nihilistic totalitarianism or cynicism respectively. I will discuss this in more detail later, since Chapter Five is the most obviously political and contemporary of the pieces. In effect this chapter deals with the impact of fracturing shared maps of meaning under the pluralistic culture of modernity, and how many individuals turned to very dark solutions to cope with it. What the right solution is never receives much attention in this book. But the answer becomes clearer later on, and looks not a little like the commitment to religious 'absolute knowing' and willing in a traditionalist reading of *Phenomenology;* with the fully wise individual reconciling himself to the world through recognizing the necessity of all that is. Aided of course by traditional religion and the state.

I have no intention here of devoting significant attention to the first two chapters of *Maps of Meaning*. This is because a discussion of processes of cognition, evolutionary psychology and epistemology go beyond the scope of this text. So I will simply devote a few paragraphs to it before moving on to more germane topics. Moreover, I personally sympathize with the description of cognition given by Peterson, though as I shall briefly explore, it is subject to both descriptive and moral critiques.

As a cognitive pragmatist myself, I largely agree with Peterson that human cognition emerged to service practical ends. That is, we focused on developing hypotheses about the nature of the world which would allow us to most effectively achieve the outcomes set for us first by instinct and, at a more evolved level, eventually by rational deliberation. As we became more capable of rational deliberation, human beings came to enjoy significant evolutionary advantages over other creatures who were primarily driven by instinct. To give a helpful example discussed in Peterson's 2016 lecture series on *Maps of Meaning,* consider the difference between an animal driven primarily by instinct to pursue certain ends and a human being who can conceptualize about different ends and deliberate on which to choose. The animal is effectively set on a single course, which may end in success or (more likely) death. But a human can run 'simulations' in their mind about potential courses of action and weigh which ones are most worth pursuing. Now this of course doesn't always result in the right choice being made. In fact, the roots of evil for Peterson lie precisely in the fact that we may know the right thing to do but choose to do the wrong thing instead, even for its own sake. But at a surface level this seems like a significant evolutionary advantage that distinguishes the cognition of human beings and potentially a handful of other species from animals with simpler brains. As the Pittsburgh Hegelian Robert Brandom might put it, the overall level of 'sapience' a species enjoys determines the range and complexity of ends they can cognitively reflect and then act upon.

The most significant gap in Peterson's analysis is that his argument is primarily an account of 'what consciousness does' rather than what—if anything—consciousness is and how it emerged. In particular consciousness is effectively an evolutionary mechanism to pursue our ends. This is a fine claim, but it appears quite vulnerable to the accusation figures like David Chalmers in *The Conscious Mind* or Thomas Nagel in 'What is it Like to Be a Bat?' direct against the materialist philosophers of mind like Davidson; that their account of an ends pursuing mechanism misses how it 'feels' to be a conscious being relative to a mechanical process. To give an example cited in Peterson's lecture, compare being a human to being a brainless sea sponge. If the only difference between us is that a brain is a better instrument for pursuing a plurality of different ends than a brainless sea sponge which is bound to pursuing one (food...mmmm), then the distinction between consciousness and non-consciousness is reduced to a matter of mechanical sophistication.

Peterson partly compensates for these theoretical difficulties by appealing to the vaguely defined phenomenological tradition of Heidegger, Husserl and others. But this doesn't adequately explain how the competing traditions of pragmatism, phenomenology, not to mention evolutionary biology and (eventually) a Jungian theory of the self, all join together into a unified theory of consciousness. There is more than a little fast and loose declaration when Peterson tries to stitch these competing traditions together, and a more sustained analysis of the differences between them would be very helpful. More foundational, this ends pursuing conception of consciousness also evades the critical problem of the 'source of the self'. To give an example, in *Reasons and Persons* the late Derek Parfit offered some highly critical arguments against the very existence of the self, contending that it could not be explained by appealing to either our body, the existence of a soul, the existence of the brain, or even our memories. Now Peterson might respond to such an objection in an existential manner by saying that it is precisely our choices about actions that constitute selfdom over time. But then what is it that is performing actions. Is it simply a relational strange loop as Douglas Hofstadter might have put it in *Godel, Escher, Bach* or is it as Kierkegaard (Anti-Climacus) put it in *The Sickness Unto Death:* 'the self is a relation which relates itself to its own self?' These are not purely speculative questions either, since what one means by the self can have foundational consequences for politics, particularly if you want to argue for a kind of liberal individualism like Peterson.

Politically this mechanical view of what consciousness does has certain consequences. It means that people are primarily defined by what they do, with a special emphasis on the ends they choose to pursue. Comparatively little emphasis is placed on what Christine Korsgaard might call the value each person intrinsically places on their life, almost by necessity. This point is also made in a different way by Heidegger, though Peterson occasionally underplays this point relative to his existential analytic of how people act in the world. Heidegger claims that before any action takes place people must 'care' about their life; it is our existential primordiality to care about our own existence and indeed existence in general. These points focus our attention away from what people do, whether in the workplace or elsewhere, and more on the intrinsic value of each person's life to themselves. The moral and political theory that seems allied to this would be that if each person intrinsically values their life, and this care is the foundation of all our values, there is something unusual about granting greater moral weight to some people than others. A wealthy white businessman does not value his life more than a poor black mother, and focusing too much attention on the success the former achieved and the latter failed to achieve distracts from efforts to ensure everyone gets equal bang for their life buck.

I will come back to this point later, but for now we have to move into the murkier realm of how society operates.

The Idealist Dialectic between Order and Chaos Part One: Theoretical Overview

The most basic distinction presented by Jordan Peterson, one which finds mature theoretical expression in *Maps of Meaning* and is practically instantiated in *12 Rules for Life: An Antidote to Chaos,* is between Order and Chaos. Indeed, oftentimes the dialectical relationship between Order and Chaos seems to approximate the 'more than metaphysical' way that beliefs both 'make' and 'are' the world. Unfortunately for such fundamental dialectical distinction the ontological status of Order and Chaos is never entirely clear. At points, particularly earlier in the book, Order and Chaos seem to be normative categories related to an individual's subjective expectations about their personal life. For instance, Peterson recounts numerous stories-likely drawing from his experience as a psychotherapist—about individuals with an 'ideal' future in mind that fractures in reality. They are then forced to confront the possibilities of their life with greater anxiety, but also freedom. Chaos therefore seems rather like what Kierkegaard described as 'dizziness' of freedom authentically experienced in *The Concept of Dread.* At other points Chaos and Order seem like more than just normative categories related to expectations in one's personal life. They seem like epistemological categories referring to what can be known by human reason, and what remains forever to us. In his paper 'The Meaning of Meaning' for *The Positive Psychology of Meaning and Spirituality,* Peterson seems to suggest that the level of expectations and epistemology are fused, allowing the individual to mediate the distinction between Order and Chaos.

Once we get past these two levels and their mediation—or 'integrated interaction'—we move onto how the distinction between Order and Chaos is represented in the inter-subjective codification in various symbols, like the flag, the nation and so on. How we move to this level is, as I will shortly discuss, a bit of a mystery. These codified symbols signify that one is in 'explored territory' where the world has been ordered within our control, or else they signify the unknown of the anomalous 'unexplored territory'. These reified symbols of collectively apprehended and projected Order and Chaos take on a huge number of forms, many of which are indexed at various points throughout *Maps of Meaning*. The best definition of Order (the Known) and Chaos (and the unknown), and their intermediary is given a fair way through Chapter Two. I will quote it at length since it is quite foundational:

The unknown is unexplored territory, naturel the unconscious, Dionysian force, the id, the Great Mother Goddess, the queen, the matrix, the matriarch, the contained, the object to be fertilized, the object to be fertilized, the source of all things, the strange, the unconscious (not a typo, it appears twice), the sensual, the foreigner, the place of return and rest, the maw of the earth, the belly of the beast, the dragon, the evil stepmother, the deep, the fecund, the pregnant, the valley, the cleft, the cave, hell, death and the grave, the moon (ruler of the night and the mysterious dark), uncontrollable emotion, matter and the earth. Any story that makes any allusion to any of these phenomena instantly involves all of them...The knower is the creative explorer, the ego, the I, the eye, the phallus, the plow, the subject, consciousness, the illuminated our enlightened one, the trickster, the fool, the hero, the coward, spirit (as opposed to matter, as opposed to dogma), the sun, son of the unknown and the known (son of the Great Mother and the Great Father). The central character in a story must play the role of hero or deceiver, must represent the sun (or, alternatively, the adversary—the power that eternally opposes the dominion of light).

The known is explored territory, culture, Apollonian control, superego, the conscience, the rational, the king, the patriarch, the wise old man and the tyrant, the giant, the ogre, the cyclops, order and authority and the crushing weight of tradition, dogma, the day sky, the countryman, the island, the heights, the ancestral spirits and the activity of the dead. Authority and its danger play central roles in interesting tales, because human society is hierarchical; and because the organized social world is omnipresent.

This associates a huge amount of material into three basic categories of Order, Chaos and the central position occupied by a heroic figure. Like the Bible, Hegel and Freud before him Peterson uses a tripartite structure to divide the world, with Order and Chaos being fundamentally in conflict and our goal in life—perhaps in existence generally—becomes to mediate between them. Unfortunately, unlike other idealists such as Hegel and Freud, Peterson does not develop a sufficiently sophisticated theoretical structure to explain how Order and Chaos are dialectically mediated at different points in the analysis. Or, to invoke his favoured terminology in the 2016 lectures, it is not philosophically clear at all how all the various confrontations between the two are mediated at different 'levels of resolution'. The book operates rather like the quoted paragraph; with a confrontation between various symbolic manifestations of the known and unknown, the dragon and the tyrannical king, the foreigner and the flag of the nation all being cited at various points without much in the way of philosophical (or really much of any) clarity on why these are all instantiations of the same phenomena. Some work is done by the earlier chapters, which suggest it is about moving from individuated to 'shared' maps of meaning. But Chapter Three on the 'adoption' of a shared map is barely 15 pages long, and basically asserts that the shared map emerges due to a 'philosophical apprenticeship' of a youth in a given 'culturally-determined historical structure'. This is an important point so I will indulge in a brief digression here.

Things become somewhat better when one looks at Peterson's more extensive scientific work on the field of ideology, belief systems and psychology. Much of this pertains to politics and so is helpful in sussing out his beliefs about how these mediations take place. For instance Peterson's co-authored paper 'Spiritual Liberals and Religious Conservatives' presents an interesting account of the association between different approaches to the divine and political orientation, finding that liberals tend to be universalistic and spiritual and conservatives traditionalists and religious. The paper 'Creative Exploration and Its Illnesses' links creativity to the capacity to apprehend more of the 'thing in itself' without ceding critical intelligence. But each of these approaches focus largely at the level of the individual and their psychological and idealized relationship to belief systems. There is very little engagement with any sociological work analysing the material practices of life and human interactions, which could help specify a great deal. These practices are presented as though they emerge largely from the 'taxonomy of personality traits in (individual) psychology' which generates an openness or closure to new experience. Such an approach is fundamentally limited and not always well described in *Maps of Meaning*. So one can understand, for instance, why individuals who are more easily 'disgusted' might become more politically conservative. But that doesn't do much to explain why Canadian conservatives support state funded health care, and Republicans in the United States oppose it at every turn. A DIGI model might explain why people have a psychological 'orientation' to favour 'one side of the political spectrum over the other'. But it tells us little about why we have decided to frame the complexities of the political compass on a binary established in eighteenth-century Revolutionary France, which might in turn tell us a great deal about the specific normative content of concrete political ideologies. Nor does it tell us anything about who is right in these disputes.

Now my point in this is not to criticize psychology — individual or social — or to suggest it has nothing to teach us about politics. First, I am no expert in either field. More importantly, I feel any claim that psychology has little to teach us about politics would be manifestly untrue; such disciplines are massively useful at a given 'level or resolution'. But they become less useful the more concrete and specific phenomena are, especially when the philosophical relationship between the various levels is not developed with a great deal of rigour or care. Much could be improved if Peterson were to spend even a modicum of time looking at the extensive historical, theoretical and sociological literature on these subjects. Unfortunately, little has improved in that regard since *Maps of Meaning*. One still gets keypad grindingly vague and ego driven comments like the following from Peterson's 2019 Op ed in the *National Post*, 'Gender Politics Has No Place in The Classroom':

Worse is the insistence characteristic of the bill (Bill C-16), the policies associated with it, and the tenth-rate academic dogmas driving the entire charade, that 'identity' is something solely determined by the individual in question (whatever that identity might be). Even sociologists (neither the older, classical, occasionally useful type, nor the modern, appalling, and positively counterproductive type) don't believe this. They understand that identity is a social role, which means that it is by necessity socially negotiated. And there's a reason for this. An identity—a role—is not merely what you think you are, moment to moment, or year by year, but, as the Encyclopedia Britannica has it (specifically within its sociology section), 'a comprehensive pattern of behavior that is socially recognized, providing a means of identifying and placing an individual in society,' also serving 'as a strategy for coping with recurrent situations and dealing with the roles of others (e.g., parent-child roles)'.

The arrogance displayed here—with no actual academics or figures cited but lots of ranting about 'tenth-rate' academic dogmas and 'positively counterproductive' sociologists—is more worthy of Kanye West than a serious academic. Given he thinks they're worthy scholarly sources for an understanding of an entire field, one is tempted to point Peterson to the dictionary subheading 'petulant' and the *Encyclopedia Britannica's* articles on 'pride'. And to point out that in most mythological parables, pride comes before a steep fall.

The Idealist Dialectic between Order and Chaos Part Two: The Divine Father and the Great Mother

This digression on the lack of philosophical clarity concerning the various 'levels' of resolution, particularly the inter-subjective social level, carries forward when it comes to looking at the particularity of various forms of symbolic coding in various cultures and traditions. We get little in the way of actually philosophically or historically defining how Order and Chaos are instantiated in all of these particular symbolic forms, let alone how if one invokes one of these forms one 'instantly involves all of them'. Nothing of great substance on how one moves from individual to shared meaning outside the realm of individual and social psychology, which any 'tenth-rate' sociologist could probably speak a lot about. And as we shall see things get even more mysterious when Peterson moves to discussing political concepts with a great deal of academic scholarship surrounding them, such as the idea of 'natural rights'. We will ignore these juicy problems for now and simply move on to the most important symbolic instantiations of Order, Chaos and the mediation between them in *Maps of Meaning* — the conflict between the Great Father and Mother and its temporary resolution by the heroic 'revolutionary' son.

This conflict is spelled out in various places in the book, particularly the lion's share of Chapter Two and the whole of Chapter Four. Peterson analyses a broad variety of world myths, ranging from the Mesopotamian creation story the *Enuma Elish* to large swathes of the Biblical Old and New Testaments. According to Peterson each of these 'primordial' myths is characterized by a confrontation between Order and Chaos, often taking the form of the Great Father and the Great Mother. In most cases the hero of the story is neither of these figures. It is instead the 'revolutionary son' who simultaneously both destroys and re-consecrates the old order. The villain in the tale depends on whether the societies which develop the myth happen to be tilting too much towards Order or too much back to Chaos. Order which becomes too overpowering transforms into tyranny and requires the heroic figure to overthrow the 'Great Father' embodying authority to liberate the people. Chaos which consumes too much requires the great hero to emerge as a lawgiver and father of his people. In the most resonant myths, for instance the Book of Exodus, the heroic figure may even fulfil both functions. In Exodus, God sends Moses to liberate the Hebrews from the Egyptians. After Pharaoh refuses to let God's chosen people go, Moses brings chaos to Egypt in the form of ten plagues. After the last of them wipes out the first-born children of the Egyptians, Pharaoh relents and lets the

Hebrews go (temporarily). After crossing the divided Red Sea and destroying Pharaoh's pursuing army, Moses then ascends up Mount Sinai for a long while, after which he delivers God's Ten Commandments to the Israelites (and delivers a short plug for the National Rifle Association).

What is interesting about such accounts for Peterson is their narrative and affective power, and the fact that similar tales abound in a wide variety of different cultures. This superficially seems true, but is also questionable. For instance, Peterson will often compare the myth of the Buddha (the 'greatest' work of Eastern mythology to his mind) with the Biblical tradition. But this conceals substantial philosophical and theological differences between the two traditions, for instance on the aforementioned nature of the self. For those operating in the Judeo-Christian tradition, the 'self' is emphatically what matters in life. It must be dedicated to God, and in many iterations of the ontotheology will exist immortally after death in a perfectly ordered world. For Buddhists, the self is the illusion which can only disappear through proper dedication to the 'Noble Eightfold Path' where one will achieve nirvana and ultimately liberation from the endless cycle of samsara, where one is reincarnated. To use Petersonian terminology, non-existence and chaos are the ends of life for Buddhists. Ignoring these differences is symptomatic of the lack of normative specificity in Peterson's work that will become frustrating very quickly. There is nothing wrong with trying to find overlapping elements to various mythological stories, but simply brushing aside the differences between them in favour of a militant universalism is unconvincing.

The more persistent problem for Peterson in *Maps of Meaning* is the lack of normative specificity demonstrated by these imagistic accounts of moral struggle. The sheer volume of mythic data assembled by Peterson is undoubtedly impressive, as is the passion with which it is examined. The problem is there is very little insight concerning what particular lessons one should draw from these tales. At most one takes away that we must aspire to be the revolutionary son by achieving some form of social balance between the orderly Divine Father and the chaotic Great Mother, and that failing to achieve this balance will have calamitous consequences. That may be so, but then what form or forms will this balance take? Should it mean a society of individualists who look after themselves, or a society of Good Samaritans ever willing to sacrifice their own interests for another? If individualist, should the political-theoretical principles underlying society be liberal, libertarian or perfectionist? If more altruistic, should goods be redistributed altruistically via some form of utilitarian universal hedonism or through a welfare state? One will find very few answers in these pages, since the only examples Peterson appeals to from real life are the extremes of communist and fascist totalitarianism which embody an extreme reaction to the divide between Order and Chaos (more on this later). In his later work Peterson becomes somewhat clearer. It is a liberal capitalist society with a strong commitment to maintaining traditions which is the society the revolutionary hero should seek to construct, though it will never be a true kingdom of heaven on earth. That is because Order and Chaos will always remain to tear at the fragile balance, and human beings will exacerbate the dissolution through acts of evil. As *12 Rules for Life* highlights, the only way to partially counter this dissolution is to urge individuals in liberal capitalist societies to focus inwardly on self-improvement.

I will discuss this depoliticization of individualism at great length later in the text so will stop here. This is in part to avoid repetition but also because this observation segues organically into perhaps the most important analysis in Peterson's entire oeuvre; the account of what constitutes evil in the world and his reading of twentieth-century totalitarianism.

The Return to Good and Evil

The most important feature of Peterson's entire oeuvre, not to mention by far the most admirable, is his treatment of the problem of evil. One often gets the sense, especially recently, that Peterson's fascination with his own celebrity lies at the core of many of his impulses. That is not the case when hearing him speak on the long litany of horrors which defined the twentieth century, and rightly made Adorno ask whether there could be poetry after Auschwitz. Any mildly feeling person cannot hear about the slaughters of the death camps, the tortures of the Gulag, the massacres in Rwanda and not feel themselves sinking into the darkness of nihilistic misanthropy. It is to Peterson's great credit that he takes the problem of evil seriously and seeks to understand it. However, as is a recurring problem, there are some substantial problems with his analysis when it moves beyond the often-theological concern with evil and into the greyer areas of historical particularity.

In *12 Rules for Life* Peterson rightly reminds us that we should never fall into the trap of suspecting that the problem of evil can be understood exclusively through an analysis of socio-political institutions and history. Evil originates with conscious beings because we, and we alone, can apprehend the suffering in the world and choose to make it worse. It takes a degree of imagination to generate not just anger, but hatred, and to direct it against the vulnerable, the powerful and even Being itself.

It does not seem reasonable to describe the young man who shot 20 children and six staff members at Sandy Hook Elementary School in Newtown, Connecticut, in 2012 as a religious person. This is equally true for the Colorado theatre gunman and the Columbine High School killers. But these murderous individuals had a problem with reality that existed at a religious depth. As one of the members of the Columbine duo wrote: 'The human race isn't worth fighting for, only worth killing. Give the Earth back to the animals. They deserve it infinitely more than we do. Nothing means anything anymore.' People who think such things view Being itself as inequitable and harsh to the point of corruption, and human Being, in particular, as contemptible. They appoint themselves supreme adjudicators of reality and find it wanting. They are the ultimate critics. The deeply cynical writer continues: 'If you recall your history, the Nazis came up with a "final solution" to the Jewish problem...Kill them all. Well, in case you haven't figured it out, I say "KILL MANKIND." No one should survive.' For such individuals, the world of experience is insufficient and evil—so to hell with everything!

Maps of Meaning relies less on such individualized anecdotes and tries to theorize the problem of evil at a more general level. Peterson frames the confrontation between good and evil as one between two hostile brothers. The first is the revolutionary son discussed before, who seeks to achieve a balance between Order and Chaos at the social level. The other is the fallen son, who Peterson regards as best archetypally expressed by the mythology of Satan. According to Peterson, the fallen son or 'adversary' comes in two forms. The first is an individual who emphasizes absolute Order and therefore tilts towards totalitarian impulses. They seek to remake the world anew with all difference and imperfection, anything that disrupts their conception or complete order, destroyed. The second is the decadent cynic, who believes that nothing matters and so we can simply give into Chaos and unbridled self and social destruction. They believe that the best world is one that is eternally burning, and their actions lay the foundation for the emergence of the totalitarian.

What then are the motivations or determinants of evil acts? Peterson wisely indicates that one cannot generalize any formula. Our imagination and creative capacity establishes the preconditions for evil, since it enables us to comprehend the suffering of others and actively seek to enhance it. This is of course a fundamentally individual development which cannot be explained through various generalizations. It needs to be examined as it develops in each person who becomes consumed by evil. Helpfully, Peterson includes a myriad of different historical and empirical examples to explain how the fall occurs. The most prominent of these are Satan, particularly as presented in the work of Milton and Goethe, and the death camps and gulags of the Nazis and Soviets. Interestingly enough, each of these corresponds in some way with the first form taken by the 'adversary'. Peterson has relatively little to say about the 'decadent' cynic who believes that nothing matters. At points he suggests that this individual is more present today than in previous years, emerging as a kind of post-modern nihilist. To infer based on his writings, I suspect Peterson would say this disposition can climatically manifest itself in the form of lone acts of tremendous violence, as demonstrated by the Columbine shooters or serial killers. Such decadents feel no desire to even coordinate acts of mass evil, since that entails a commitment to a form of Order which is antithetical to their disposition. These decadent individuals are less central to Peterson's analysis of evil than the totalitarian, so I will cease analysing them here. The sustained treatment will come in Chapter Four, where I discuss his very thin account of post-modern culture and cynicism.

The concluding chapter to *Maps of Meaning* sets itself the task of understanding death committed en masse, not simply in rogue acts of spectacular violence. Satan, Hitler and Stalin are each at first characterized by a desire—not evil in itself but even admirable—to help order the world. They become proud of their abilities, and come to see everything which exists outside of their vision of the world or comprehension as abhorrent and noxious. In such cases knowledge itself becomes a danger, since it leads one to the temptation that what a person cannot understand exists independently of their control. This gradually leads to the impetus to dominate everything and everyone.

The infernal projects of extermination, designed and carried out with such ruthless intelligence through much of the twentieth century, are the inevitable endpoint of this impetus. The lesser adversary may simply seek to dominate his family or those around him, stunted by a lack of power or ambition. But certainly truly demonic individuals like Hitler, Stalin and so on breed progeny to carry out their will, promising that once all forms of anomaly and foreignness are gone the world will have been remade into the kingdom of heaven. Of course this superficial justification is merely a screen for the far darker desire to 'revenge' oneself against Being, which is considered irreversibly chaotic and evil. So ultimately the totalitarian will swallow themselves in their hatred and violence, much as the Fuhrer himself did in 1945 when he turned his dwindling arms against the German people themselves.

Understanding this point is key for grasping Peterson's abiding anxiety about all forms of radical politics. He fears that they conceal this deeper impulse towards revenge against Being; that beneath all the slogans of a classless society and an authentic volk is a repressed but powerful resentment against existence itself, and especially the perceived victimizers, that can only manifest through attacking everything that defies control. Peterson is convinced that if these self-described radical utopians come to power, then their real motivations will become clear through an endless will to destruction. This point is of course drawn straight from Nietzsche, who more than any other philosopher theorized on the power and importance of resentment as a political emotion. At its peak the man of ressentiment masks his desire for revenge on existence itself under the auspices of overwhelming virtue. As Nietzsche put it in the third essay of the *Genealogy of Morals*:

These worm-eaten physiological casualties are all men of ressentiment, a whole, vibrating realm of subterranean revenge, inexhaustible and insatiable in its eruptions against the happy, and likewise in masquerades of revenge and pretexts for revenge: when will they actually achieve their ultimate, finest, most sublime triumph of revenge? Doubtless if they succeeded in shoving their own misery, in fact all misery, on to the conscience of the happy: so that the latter eventually start to be ashamed of their happiness and perhaps say to one another: 'It's a disgrace to be happy! There is too much misery!'...But there could be no greater or more disastrous misunderstanding than for the happy, the successful, those powerful in body and soul to begin to doubt their right to happiness in this way.

The men of ressentiment are only a few steps away from evil without knowing it. They believe that the world has mistreated and despised them, and formulate enemies who are responsible. The capitalist, the Jew, the Muslim, Western civilization, white males, heterosexuals and the heteronormative; the mere existence or presence of these individuals as contrary to what one is can be taken as proof that a person is oppressed by difference which must be exterminated in order to feel one is in a safe space. If these feelings are channelled politically, the result is oppression and the effacement of all rights and safety. Naturally Peterson regards the contemporary 'post-modern neo-Marxist' left as embodying precisely this spirit of revenge, which can only end disastrously if given full reign. Post-modern leftists are defined by its sick attachment to victimhood, and a desire to revenge themselves against all who have wronged them.

As a characterization of post-modern theorizing this is rather nonsensical, as Conrad Hamilton will show later in this book. It effectively ignores most figures considered post-modern theorists in lieu of stereotyping, and largely eschews any major engagement with the literature on post-modernity as a culture. None the less, there is something to Peterson's critique of the Left as driven by resentment. This has long been a favoured accusation of the sophisticated political right and many leftists have struggled to respond to it, though theorists like Wendy Brown in *Wounded Attachments* and Fredric Jameson in 'The Political Unconscious' have taken us a long way there. Later on I will discuss this in more detail. For now I will conclude with some final remarks on *Maps of Meaning*.

Concluding Thoughts and the Turn to Justice

Peterson's account of evil is often very interesting, and caps off *Maps of Meaning* in a satisfying manner. Unfortunately, for all its virtues, the account lacks specificity when applied to a contemporary setting. And where he has endeavoured to provide some by accusing post-modern neo-Marxists of being totalitarians in a new guise, his claims are unsubstantiated and even paranoid. This is the problem with developing such an extravagant and idealized theory concerning how 'beliefs create' and even 'are' the world. Such a theoretical enterprise will often result in an intense set of abstractions which struggle when efforts are made to concretize them. This is especially true when he endeavours to speak about specific political and social phenomena or mythological traditions. Everything tends to be assimilated into the whole, ironically with its particularity and individuality subsumed. This would be less of an egregious sin if Peterson developed a sufficiently robust philosophical account of how his theory operates at different 'levels of resolution'. Following another self-described pragmatist like Robert Brandom, who might endeavour to 'make explicit' the Hegelian style logic whereby one passes from individual consciousness, to adoption of a 'shared map of meaning', to how these shared maps instantiate themselves in specific contexts. Peterson makes some effort to do so with his work on empirical and social psychology, but the results are still highly individuated and tell us little about why specific political beliefs and institutions emerge as they do. Everything still operates at a highly idealized level, and patronizing remarks directed at sociologists and other 'tenth-rate' academics who make their living describing this level of resolution don't inspire faith that things will get better.

Curiously, nowhere does the problem of a lack of specificity become clearer than in Peterson's treatment of morality and justice. He has a great deal to say about the psychological and social contexts behind the fall into evil. Much of this is highly interesting. But when it comes to contemporary settings, Peterson falters when describing anything more than individualized instances of evil. These are more characteristic, one guesses since nowhere is this clarified, of the second form of the antagonist: the decadent who just wants to see the world burn. His frequent references to the Columbine shooters suggest they might warrant categorization in this category. But Peterson's account of the totalitarian adversary today is, as I shall discuss later, remarkably vague and even paranoid in its orientation. There is simply no other way to describe someone who would claim that a trans rights activist can be compared to a Maoist since 'the philosophy which guides their utterances is the same'.

More striking still is the complete lack of any complex theory of morality and justice in his work. Aside from the paper 'Religion, Sovereignty, Natural Rights, and the Constituent Elements of Experience' published with the *Archive for the Psychology of Religion* little systematic effort has been made to fulfil this gap. This is quite remarkable given the moralizing quality that underpins a great deal of Peterson's work. He largely seems indifferent to justice as a specific set of principles, and therefore has relatively little to explicitly say about what one ought to do in a specific situation. His advice on these points is largely concerned with psychological well-being and a certain kind of authenticity in the face of Order and Chaos. This unfortunately means that we must infer Peterson's understanding of morality and justice from his other works on different topics, which is by no means a simple or graceful task. In the next chapter, I will attempt to unpack this problem by looking at his scatted remarks on morality and in particular the account of the individual given in *12 Rules for Life*. This is the closest one can get to a moral handbook by Peterson, and so is the best resource available to answer such questions. My contention is that he implicitly argues for a kind of ordered liberty approach to political justice centred around a quasi-perfectionist moral theory. I will also show how this approach to political justice and perfectionism is in stark tension to many other principles espoused in his work.

Chapter Three

Jordan Peterson, Classical Liberalism and Conservatism

The Individual and Society

It took a long time to settle on a title 12 Rules for Life: An Antidote to Chaos. *Why did that one rise up above all others? First and foremost, because of its simplicity. It indicates clearly that people need ordering principles, and that chaos otherwise beckons. We require rules, standards, values-alone and together. We're pack animals, beasts of burden. We must bear a load to justify our miserable existence. We require routine and tradition. That's Order.*

12 Rules for Life, Introduction

If *Maps of Meaning* is a modern right Hegelian re-treading of *The Phenomenology of Spirit* then sure *12 Rules for Life: An Antidote to Chaos* is the closest Peterson will get to *The World as Will and Representation.* Where the former book discusses (or rather, philosophically passes over in silence) the passage of consciousness towards the codification of a shared map of meaning in cultural mythology, religion and literature, the latter is much more straightforwardly directed at individuals. It is also the closest Peterson comes to writing a guide to moral and sound political behaviour, though this is hardly done in a systematic manner. More often than not one gets anecdotes, references and moralism in lieu of actual moral and political analysis. Much of this is delivered at a 'lower' resolution than his earlier work, signifying Peterson's passage from academic to public intellectual with a mass following. Despite these limitations, it is important to discuss the book to truly understand why

Peterson has become so synonymous with a critique of the Left and support for conservative and/or classical liberal positions.

At the centre of *12 Rules for Life* are, surprisingly, a dozen rules to help human beings transcend the suffering Peterson argues is built into the structure of Being itself. His denotation of Being with a capital B is directly drawn from Heidegger, who was also an existentially minded thinker attracted to reactionary viewpoints. Unlike Heidegger, whom from the concluding chapters of *Being and Time* on often struggled to detach the ontological concept of Being from the limitations of phenomenological idealism, Peterson seems quite willing to interpret ontology in normative idealist terms. This has far more in common with Schopenhauer and Nietzsche than Heidegger, who as philosophers of the will were willing to give Being a normative slant similar to Peterson's. Beliefs still make and are the world in *12 Rules for Life,* while for the later Heidegger our cultural beliefs about Being are highly flawed and need to be overcome through the end of philosophy and the movement to 'thinking'. This is of course because Heidegger recognized that the course of mythologizing from Plato to Nietzsche resulted in the ultimate turn towards nihilistic modernity; which isn't something a defender of everything Western like Peterson would want to hear.

One curious aside is worth noting. Peterson is well known for moralizing about the evils of invoking Marxist philosophy after the publication of the *Gulag Archipelago* laid bare the apparently cancerous nature of Marxism. Yet he has little to say about Heidegger's participation in the Nazi Party and his unwillingness to apologize for it long after the publication of *Mans Search for Meaning.* This is quite a striking juxtaposition, since Marx died decades before Lenin ever sniffed at power, while Heidegger actively lived through the worst years of Nazi tyranny. All of the extensive debate about Heidegger's Nazism and anti-Semitism gets passed over in silence, but the Jewish Jacques Derrida (who did actually take the Heidegger issue seriously in his book *On Spirit)* gets chided for apparently trying to make Marx great again. This initiates an annoying habit of Peterson's which persists throughout the book, where the scandals of figures he admires are overlooked while (typically leftist) authors he does not admire typically get scolded for far less valid reasons than Nazis like Heidegger and anti-democratic illiberal perfectionists like Nietzsche.

Moving on from Being itself, we get to the 12 rules laid down by Peterson. These appear superficially mundane, and have therefore attracted a degree of scorn by leftist critics for their apparent banality. While I understand the inclination, the seemingly trite quality of the rules belies the (very) serious points about life and suffering Peterson is trying to get across. One might give him some credit for attempting to deliver such sermonizing rhetoric in a more humorous and down to earth fashion. The 12 rules are:

1. Stand up straight with your shoulders back.
2. Treat yourself like someone you are responsible for helping.
3. Make friends with people who want the best for you.
4. Compare yourself to who you were yesterday, not to who someone else is today.
5. Do not let your children do anything that makes you dislike them.
6. Set your house in perfect order before you criticize the world.
7. Pursue what is meaningful (not what is expedient).
8. Tell the truth—or, at least, don't lie.
9. Assume that the person you are listening to might know something you don't.
10. Be precise in your speech.
11. Do not bother children when they are skateboarding.

12. Pet a cat when you encounter one on the street.

Each one of these rules is detailed quite extensively in the book, with each one receiving a chapter's worth of explication alongside the strange Heideggerian introduction and the summative conclusion. Now as psychological advice to individuals looking to set their personal life in order, I suspect Peterson's 12 rules might be helpful to many. In particular to young men looking for such personalized guidance who are perhaps unconsciously seeking a symbolic father figure who provides tough love and stern life advice. In such circumstances Peterson may fit the bill, which should be the case given his decades of training and practical experience as a clinical psychologist. There is nothing wrong with suggesting that one make friends with people who will want the best for you, or insisting that people pet a cat they encounter on the street (my own feline is next to me while I write this, so perhaps he's biasing me). Anyone in any political or social situation would benefit from having good and reliable friends, and finding gratification in small acts of kindness. The problem isn't with such individualized psychological advice; it is with the frequently implicit and occasionally explicit political orientation which is delivered alongside the advice.

One of the inner polemics of *12 Rules for Life* is against left-wing efforts to criticize the social and economic institutions characteristic of liberal capitalist societies, or to suggest they are responsible for a great deal of suffering around the world. This is made abundantly clear in Chapter One, 'Stand up straight with your shoulders back', which includes the infamous comparison between human and lobster hierarchies. While there is nothing untoward about suggesting there is evolutionary continuity between ourselves and our crustacean brothers, the point Peterson is trying to make is that hierarchy is natural and the hierarchies of liberal capitalism in particular are to some extent inevitable and justified. Chapter Six is also significant along the same lines. Peterson insists that an individual should put one's house in 'perfect order' before criticizing the world. That interpreting this 'precisely' would mean that hardly anyone, anywhere would ever criticize the world—at least in developed countries where people are likely to read *12 Rules for Life*—is one of the intentions behind the rule.

The deeper point this reflects is that the individual and their psychological problems are ontologically and morally prior to society and its injustices. Peterson has of course felt this way for a long time; he chronicled his decision to move away from the field of politics with its 'economic' explanations for problems to psychology in the opening of *Maps of Meaning*. But much as in this earlier work, this position is never really argued for so much as asserted with a great deal of confidence. And as with *Maps of Meaning* a more philosophical and dialectical analysis of the ontological relationship between the individual and society is lacking. But at least one now gets a better sense of the moral orientation behind the position. Peterson believes that individuals must solve their personal problems first before looking outwards to try and fix what they feel is wrong with the world. Moreover they need to pay close attention to those elements of society which serve a preservative, and not let utopian schemes incline them to inadvertently put the welfare of the abstract collective ahead of the 'natural' rights of the individual. Indeed, he often implies the conceptualization of individualized natural rights against the collective was an almost sacred development which must be defended with great care. As he put it in the paper 'Religion, Sovereignty, Natural Rights, and the Constituent Elements of Experience':

> Even the chimpanzee and the wolf, driven by their biology and culture, act out the idea of sovereignty as inherent in the individual. Human beings have taken the idea much further of course. We have observed it in action and codified its

consequences. We have turned it into religion and philosophy, implicit and explicit knowledge. No matter what an individual does, in modern society—even if he is in clear violation of the law—his natural rights remain intact. No matter how outcast he is, how apparently beyond redemption, his existence may still contribute something to the whole. This is not merely a 'metaphysical' (this again...) idea. Nor can it be dismissed, regarded as merely a rational construction, without such dismissal threatening the integrity of the modern state, psychological and social.

So it becomes clear that Peterson's belief in the ontological and moral priority of the individual runs very deep. Everything in *12 Rules for Life* hinges on it, the failure of the Toronto Maple Leafs flows from ignoring it, and abandoning this more than metaphysical idea would destroy the psychological and social integrity of the modern state. This would seem to make Peterson something close to a classical liberal or even a libertarian, with his absolute insistence on the natural rights of the individual against society. But if the individual is everything, why then does Peterson show such concern for 'rules, values, standards' and 'tradition' all of which entail some commitment to maintaining collective norms of behaviour and belief?

The answer is such a hyper-modernist position would obviously not be to the liking of someone like Peterson, for whom individualistic liberalism is both a blessing to be cherished and a cross to be borne. Far more than *Maps of Meaning*, which routinely emphasized the creative importance of the 'revolutionary' son in helping society progress, *12 Rules for Life* is a far more openly conservative book. The critique of modernity central to the earlier work has evolved into a suspicion of permissiveness and occasionally almost open horror at the collapse of traditionalism and the various social hierarchies it supported. *Maps of Meaning* was the work of a younger scholar, who disliked modernity but remained highly concerned to protect the creative powers of the individual against the totalitarian impulse towards absolute order. This later book, subtitled *An Antidote to Chaos*, shifts emphasis and brings the conservative impulse for order to the fore. One sees this very clearly in Peterson's rather loose efforts to naturalize the social hierarchy in liberal capitalist societies. This brings us, inevitably, to consider the lobster.

On Lobsters and Labour: The Social Necessity of Hierarchy

The first major chapter of *12 Rules for Life* is undoubtedly the best known; and with good reason. It opens the text with a quirky, but telling, comparison between the dominance hierarchies of lobsters and those of human beings. The purported ambition of the chapter is to demonstrate the salience of Peterson's rule that one should 'stand up straight with your shoulders back'. But as we shall see the more implicit intention goes considerably deeper than a bit of well-meaning advice about posture like your mother might have given you.

Peterson points out the lobsters, like almost all animals we know of, have a compulsive need to 'establish dominance'. This is paralleled by the evolution of practices and features to demonstrate submission, which is useful in enabling non-dominant members to survive violent encounters with their more assertive and powerful kin. Peterson recounts how lobsters, if moved to a new territory they are unfamiliar with, will invariably approach it through cautious exploration. If frightened, they will quickly seek shelter in the nearest available place to hide. This is obviously a significant advantage on the ocean floor, but it comes at a price. Other lobsters will also be on the lookout for premium shelters. They are also on the lookout for food and mates. Lobsters frequently encounter one another while exploring for these goods, and will quickly perform certain defensive or aggressive behaviours. These include releasing a spray which will inform other lobsters of their sex, size, health and mood. Smaller and more passive lobsters will frequently back down from conflict with larger ones, displaying behaviour like retreating in the face of their counterpart. More aggressive lobsters may get into a standoff, engaging in behaviour to assert dominance over the other. This can include moving antennae, advancing in a dangerous manner, and folding their claws downward. In the event that both lobsters feel especially roided up that day, they will engage in combat. Success is achieved when one lobster flips its opponent on its back, in which case the losing lobster will retreat. In some extreme instances, even this will not stop the horror and the lobsters will fight until there is a clear winner and loser. Typically the loser, and sometimes even the winner, do not survive the trial by combat. Interestingly, the story does not stop here. Peterson notes that such combat changes the brain chemistry of both the winner and the loser, determined by the output of serotonin and octopamine modulating communication between lobster neurons. Winning a fight increases the amount of the former chemical relative to the latter, while the opposite is true for the loser. The social result is that lobsters who win fights tend to have higher levels of serotonin, which makes them more assertive and confident. Lobsters who lose have higher levels of octopamine, which makes them more likely to act 'defeated looking, scrunched up, inhibited, drooping, [and] skulking'. Those lobsters who have won a fight are also more likely to win the next one, while losing lobsters become more likely to fail in their quest for dominance.

This is all fascinating marine biology in its own right, but what might it be doing in a chapter about human psychology? Peterson's point becomes immediately clear right after this tidy summation. There is an evolutionary continuity between lobsters and humans which apparently explains many features of our own social world. But of course Peterson is not simply concerned to explain these continuities, but to justify 'the ways of God to man'. And in his opinion hierarchy is natural and inevitable. Moreover, it will frequently be stark and brutal, with immense spoils going to winners and the losers. But this is acceptable to Peterson since, as he points out, the exceeding lobster hierarchies are 'exceedingly stable'.

It isn't hard to infer the moral and political lesson Peterson intends us to learn. If anything, he is very transparent about it in the same section:

It's winner-take-all in the lobster world, just as it is in human societies, where the top 1 per cent have as much loot as the bottom 50 per cent — and where the richest 85 people have as much as the bottom three and a half billion. That same brutal principle of unequal distribution applies outside the financial domain — indeed, anywhere that creative production is required. The majority of scientific papers are published by a very small group of scientists. A tiny proportion of musicians produces almost all the recorded commercial music. Just a handful of authors sell all the books...

Peterson then goes on to further vindicate this principle by appealing to economic theory and the Bible. He refers to Price's Law, named after the economist Derek J. Price, and the arguments of Vilfredo Pareto. He also discusses the 'Matthew Principle' which refers to Jesus's statement in Matthew 25: 29 that 'to those who have everything, more will be given; from those who have nothing, everything will be taken'. This is a rather tacky reference to a bastardized Biblical principle, given that Christ was invoking a parable to discuss the importance of storing up moral virtue in preparation for the day of his return. This virtue would be demonstrated in part by looking after the 'least' amongst us, including the hungry, the thirsty and the foreign. As Jesus puts it later in Matthew 25.

Then the King will say to those on his right, 'Come, you who are blessed by My Father, inherit the kingdom prepared for you from the foundation of the world. For I was hungry and you gave me something to eat, I was thirsty and you gave me something to drink, I was a stranger and you took me in, I was naked and you clothed me, I was sick and you looked after me, I was in prison and you visited me.' Then the righteous will answer Him, 'Lord, when did we see you hungry and feed you, or thirsty and give you something to drink? When did we see you a stranger and take You in, or naked and clothe you? When did we see you sick or in prison and visit you?' And the King will reply, 'Truly I tell you, whatever you did for one of the least of these brothers of Mine, you did for me.'

This is not the last place where Peterson will make a mockery of Christian doctrine by invoking its tropes to reinforce his admiration for social hierarchy. But it is one of the more ironic given he invokes the so-called Matthew Principle with scarcely an acknowledgement for what Jesus actually means.

In either case, Peterson goes on in the rest of the chapter to illustrate the variety of ways that human beings perform dominance or submissiveness in their interpersonal relations and linking these propensities to the generation of the stratified social and economic hierarchies we are all intimately familiar with today. The normative take away is that it is better to strive to be at the top of the pecking order than to find oneself at the bottom, and Peterson provides a variety of tips on how to achieve this goal. These include everything on how to appear more dominant, and thus attractive, towards the opposite sex, how to delay gratification in the moment for more enduring success later, and how to posture correctly by standing up straight with the shoulders back. Once a relative level of dominance and success is achieved, it becomes easier to maintain in no small part because like the lobster our brains will become hardwired to regard ourselves as successful people. The one thing we should not do is start blaming the existence of hierarchies on cultural or political factors, as Peterson tiresomely emphasizes.

> All that matters from the Darwinian perspective is permanence—and the dominance hierarchy, however social and cultural it might appear, has been around for some half a billion years. It's permanent. It's real. The dominance hierarchy is not capitalism. It's not communism either for that matter. It's not the military industrial complex. It's not the patriarchy—that disposable, arbitrary, malleable cultural artefact. It's not even a human creation; not in the most profound sense. It is instead a near-eternal aspect of the environment, and much of what is blamed on these more ephemeral manifestations is a consequence of its unchanging existence.

This sentence nicely encapsulates Petersonian morality in a nutshell. There is an implicit fear of efforts to break up dominance hierarchies by conceptualizing them as 'malleable'; in particular economic, military and gendered hierarchies. By insisting that dominance hierarches are 'near-eternal' 'unchanging' and so on, Peterson insulates existing hierarchies from substantial criticism by naturalizing them. This helps preserve the 'order' he puts so much stock in, even when present amongst the lobsters, and ensures that the exercise of individual freedom is never directed towards potentially destabilizing efforts to transform overarching social structures associated with illegitimate dominance hierarchies. Instead the exercise of freedom is directed towards self-improvement that will allow the fortunate few to climb to the top of the dominance hierarchy. How this benefits everyone else is never really explicated in much detail throughout 12 Rules for Life. The closest I can infer based on

Peterson's varied comments about competence, intelligence and hierarchy is he believes that a system where the best or at least more competent will rise to the top will ultimately work to the benefit of all through establishing a more productive and orderly society. This is of course a classic argument of moralistic defenders of unbridled liberal capitalism, from Ayn Rand through to Rand Paul.

So what to make of all this? First one should note that, despite Peterson's denunciation of figures who blame all dominance hierarchies on culture and politics, that no one I am familiar with has ever blamed all dominance hierarchies on culture and politics. This includes even the most egalitarian thinkers on the Left. This is perhaps why Peterson is unable to single out a specific individual who holds such a bizarre conception. Certainly some of Peterson's favourite targets did not. Marx was well aware of evolutionary biology, and positively referenced Darwin's theory of competitive evolution as a precursor to his own dialectical approach to history (though he was critical of Darwin for allegedly reading bourgeois values into the animal kingdom). Nowhere does Marx ever claim that the natural world is anything less than a competitive and antagonistic place, and he often points out that human history has almost always been the same. Feminist theorists like Simone de Beauvoir never denied that there was obviously a biological basis for the initial emergence of gendered divisions of labour; for instance the superior physical strength of males relative to females in hunter-gatherer societies lead to men enjoying greater independence while hunting. But they also argued that these practices quickly assumed ideological and cultural forms to justify the unnecessary and unjust oppression of women. The position of the various post-modern theorists is more complex, but certainly someone like Michel Foucault never argued that dominance hierarchies and the influence of power can ever be eliminated. Indeed Foucault often went out of his way to stress the productive qualities of power and hierarchy in varied contexts; for instance by guiding children to adulthood safely.

What critics attack is therefore not the necessity of hierarchy in general, but particular hierarchies that are unjustifiable. These may have some roots in our natural inclinations, but the specific form they assume in society is regarded as a deviation from a superior or more just alternative. To give one example, Rawlsian liberals and many social democrats argue that economic hierarchies and inequality can justifiably exist, but only if they are fair and demonstrably work to the primary benefit of the least well off. A more radical push against economic hierarchy came from Marx, but even the Marxists never called for the achievement of full equality along all dimensions of life. Indeed Marx was highly critical of the socialist calls for abstract equality between all persons, regarding it as ahistorical and utopian. Instead Marx wanted the elimination of class-based hierarchies in particular, since he regarded them as emerging from exploitative material conditions we would be better off leaving behind. Or to look at the feminist example, liberal feminists like Martha Nussbaum and even radicals like Catharine MacKinnon in no way seek to eliminate all forms of social hierarchy. This is in part because they believe the superior authority vested in legal institutions and actors can be exercised to eliminate patriarchal forms of oppression. And the list goes on. Now one might object to any or all of these calls to eliminate specific hierarchies, but the point is that none of the figures mentioned wanted to eliminate hierarchy in general. Addressing their arguments means looking at whether the specific hierarchies they want dissolved serve a useful function, not making extremely vague claims about how hierarchy of some sort or another will always exist.

Of course we will never get around to actually doing this because Peterson insists continuously that concern with social injustices should always be secondary to caring for our private self. This brings us to the next significant chapter in *12 Rules for*

Life, about putting one's life in complete order before trying to change the world.

Cleaning One's Room before Putting the World in Order

Alongside Chapter One the most important political ruminations in *12 Rules for Life* appear in Chapter Six, 'Set Your House in Perfect Order Before You Criticize the World'. This is a theme Peterson comes back to quite consistently, particularly with regard to youthful social justice advocates. This is also the chapter where Peterson's inclinations towards a Burkean-style ordered liberty approach to politics become most transparent. He continuously insists that the complexity of the world is so vast that individuals who do not fully even have their own lives in order have no right to assume they can improve it. Far better to adopt the cautious approach of conforming to the expectations of the external social world, while working to develop one's self-worth and success from within.

Peterson's justification for this position is in fact highly consonant with the cautious and even pessimistic conservative philosophies articulated by figures like Leo Strauss, Russell Kirk and others. Though as always, political dimensions of such inclinations are less explicitly brought to the surface than in the work of those seminal thinkers. Chapter Six opens with a chilling analysis of the Columbine killers' motivation, echoing the concluding sections of *Maps of Meaning* on the problem of evil. He points out how the killers appointed themselves judges of existence itself, and the human race in particular, and found them wanting. Their response was to take revenge against existence through a spectacularly impotent act of violence. Peterson points out that these figures, and evil in general, emerge because life in the world is invariably hard. Like the pessimistic conservative Schopenhauer before him, at points Peterson comes very close to accepting the wisdom of Silenus: that the best thing in life would be to have never been born, and the next best thing would be to die quickly. As Peterson puts it early in the chapter:

> Life is in truth very hard. Everyone is destined for pain and slated for destruction. Sometimes suffering is clearly the result of a personal fault such as willful blindness, poor decision-making or malevolence. In such cases, when it appears to be self-inflicted, it may even seem just. People get what they deserve, you might contend. That's cold comfort, however, even when true. Sometime, if those who are suffering changed their behavior, then their lives would unfold less tragically. But human control is limited. Susceptibility to despair, disease, aging and death is universal.

Given all this, it is understandable that some people may come away from the evils of life with a desire to do great evil themselves. But Peterson also points out that some may emerge from even tremendous tragedy without being defined by resentment and anger. They may come away with the conviction to do good, though what that means is not necessarily being good to others immediately or even indefinitely.

Instead we should recognize that life inevitably involves suffering, and do our best to mitigate it for ourselves before we take any significant strides towards eliminating alleged socio-political and economic causes of harm. What does this entail? It means taking care of the 'small things' in our life and recognizing the opportunities we have available to us. We should focus on issues such as are you working 'hard on you career, or even your job, or are you letting bitterness and resentment drag you down?' Am I treating my loved ones with care? Am I taking care of my responsibilities? Am I trying to 'make things around (me) better?' If I am not doing all I can to perfect myself in these local areas then I have no business attempting to blame anyone or anything else for what I am going through. Am I saying or doing things that make me 'weak and ashamed' or am I only saying and doing things that make me 'strong?' It also means not just using our judgement, but recognizing the contributions of our 'culture' and that the 'wisdom of the past' passed on by our 'dead ancestors' has useful things to teach us. As Peterson puts it in the conclusion to the short chapter: 'Don't blame capitalism, the radical Left (thanks), or the iniquity of your enemies. Don't reorganize the state until you have ordered your own experience. Have some humility? If you cannot bring peace to your household, how dare you try to rule a city? Let your own soul guide you.'

If we accomplish this task, our soul will become 'less corrupted' and able to bear the inescapable tragedy of life without it degenerating into 'outright hellishness'. Our anxiety, hopelessness and resentment and anger may recede. We will see our existence as 'genuine good' even in the face of our own vulnerability and perhaps even become a more prominent example for others. Our ability to set our house in order will inspire others to strive to make the world a better place. This mantra that caring for yourself first and foremost is indirectly caring for others is not unique to this chapter. Peterson also brings up this point in another bastardization of Biblical principles, when he claims in the Coda that the proper response to the poor man's plight is to strive through right example to be an inspiration to him. Or how he insists that Jesus's efforts to show compassion to the prostitutes and sinners indicates only that he is the perfect man, while our own ambitions to improve their lot are motivated by a desire to 'draw attention to...inexhaustible reserves of compassion and good will'. In each circumstance the proper interpretation of Christian doctrine is apparently, do what one can, but only after looking after yourself first and if it is expedient and undemonstrative.

When you boil it down, Peterson's positions on these points often look like little more than a jazzed-up variant of WASPY wisdom. Our first obligations are always to ourselves and to those immediately around us. If something is going wrong, then it is likely either natural or we ourselves are to blame for it. Even if there may be cause to combat injustice, we should only do so if we have put our own life into order first. Criticizing such a position isn't especially hard. The underpinning logic of this chapter is that there exists a tension between looking after one's own life and engaging in political efforts to rectify injustices. But this by no means seems clear to me.

First, Peterson largely ignores that—while the existence of suffering generally may indeed transcend politics and be ineradicable—the specific cause of someone's suffering may well have political and economic roots. Consider Peterson's typical denunciation of the resentment people may feel throughout their career or in their job. As I pointed out in Chapter Two, invoking and criticizing unhappiness in the workplace as 'resentment' is a fairly typical approach by conservative authors. What it misses is, as Fredric Jameson points out in his critique of Nietzsche, that people may have justifiable reasons to be angry at the structural conditions of their workplace which hold them back. This can take a huge number of different forms. A Marxist might point out that one can feel exploited if the value created by my labour is appropriated by others for little compensation; for instance how Wal Mart employees are paid minimum wage while the Walton family enjoys hundreds of billions worth of inherited wealth. A Rawlsian might point out that someone who is inhibited from advancing their socio-economic status because they were born into a poor family might well criticize a social system which does not ameliorate these conditions, but offers tremendous advantages to those born into affluent circumstances. Dismissing these concerns about exploitation and unfairness as mere resentment is highly reductive, and demanding that figures in such circumstances just focus on their own life ignores that the basis of their problems rests in injustices we have moral responsibilities to end.

Peterson may reply that even if all this was granted people will still be better off just trying to improve their lot than rectifying such titanic problems. But this brings me to my second point. Many people may well resolve their problems through 'criticizing' and changing the world, and as an added point they would also resolve these problems for others rather than just themselves. The aforementioned person who feels exploited at work may do a great service to themselves and others by starting a union; an act which can take a great deal of courage in today's corporate climate. Someone concerned with their 'health and well-being' may indeed be advised to quit their bad habits. They might also demand things like access to superior taxpayer funded healthcare. They might point out that two huge predictors of engaging in the aforementioned bad habits—everything from smoking to eating bad food to excessive substance abuse—are a lack of education, and poverty. So perhaps much can be gained by improving education and taking efforts to end poverty beyond just serving as an example to the poor. An individual who wants to treat their spouse and children with 'dignity and respect' might respond that this is exceptionally difficult to do given the stresses of precarious employment, stagnating or declining real wages, and the blurring of the work/life divide under the conditions of technological change.

Peterson has little to say on these issues, which may appear more mundane than reflection upon the soul. But this very lack of engagement is quite telling. It isn't that Peterson is disinterested in issues of redistribution and political agitation, instead focusing on individual human psychology and efforts. Instead he wants a focus on individual human psychology and efforts to be the aim of politics. Individuals can make efforts and strive to become personally better off, but individuals should not make efforts and strive to make society better off except in extremely qualified circumstances. This is deeply reflective of the implicit but pervasive conservative ordered liberty approach to politics underpinning much of Peterson's advice on how to live well.

This chapter is also where some of the major theoretical tensions in Peterson's work emerge, though these are very rarely explicated clearly. This is perhaps for the best, since when they bubble up they reveal a more disturbing dimension to his work. Peterson consistently situates his work in a mélange of Judeo-Christian traditionalism and liberalism, which despite his protestations in Chapter Eleven about having some left-wing views, is very consonant with middle of the road North American conservatism. One is almost tempted to label it a form of neo-Fusionism. But there is also a darker dimension to his work that is more interesting, but also highly problematic. In *12 Rules for Life* Peterson shares little of the optimism that occasionally emerges in the work of fusionist thinkers like Frank Meyer or William Buckley, who emphasized the creative potential of freedom and the joys that flowed from Christian grace. While the emphasis on individual creativity occasionally spruced up *Maps of Meaning,* by the twenty-first century Peterson often gives into the kind of reactionary pessimism well criticized by Corey Robin in *The Reactionary Mind.* At these points Peterson comes very close to leaping past the Christian tradition and into what is sometimes referred to as perfectionism. He consistently invokes the Schopenhauerean-Nietzschean trope that the most important thing is to strengthen the self against the suffering of the world. The stronger one becomes, the greater and more worthy of respect and emulation by those around. This is of course dramatically in contrast to the Christian tradition Peterson invokes elsewhere, as both Schopenhauer and Nietzsche well knew. Jesus would not likely insist, as Peterson does in Chapter Eleven, that compassion can be a vice. The Lamb of God we are to imitate would never resent people for 'walking all over' him. In fact one suspects the truth of Christianity lies much closer to

Shusaku Endo's interpretation in his classic novel *Silence*. When a believer is faced with having to trample on an icon of Christ to save dozens of believing Christians, Jesus' voice rings out after years of silence to proclaim: 'Trample, trample. It is to be trampled on by you that I am here.'

This tension in Peterson's thinking points to what is darkest in his work. What Peterson puts forward in these moments isn't so much a kind of fusionism, as an effort to blend Nietzschean doctrines about superior people and an admiration of strength and power with a form of Christian traditionalism. He is of course not the first to aspire to draw from both wells; they were quite common in right and far-right circles in early twentieth-century Europe. Like Peterson, critics such as T.S. Eliot and Carl Schmitt often shared the modernist admiration of the strong and wilful individual on the one hand while drawing on traditionalism to castigate the materialism and nihilism of the modern era. They also shared Peterson's distaste for social agitation and efforts to achieve greater equality, combining the elitist's disdain for the mass with the snob's appeal to historical authority. Underpinning each of these theories was of course a tremendous fear, often framed in the same apocalyptic language framed in *12 Rules for Life*. The world was conceived of as a dark and wicked place, and only superior men with a deep understanding of history could restore value to the world through their efforts to rise above the mass. Politically this of course meant that efforts to extend democracy too far, to tolerate too much, or to redistribute power and wealth should be looked at with extreme suspicion as a kind of levelling. The natural hierarchy is not to be upended but restored to its proper parameters. One might claim such an association is unfair, but it is hard to tell how else to interpret passages such as the following in Chapter Eleven, where Peterson explains the attraction of right-wing populism.

The populist groundswell of support for Donald Trump in

the US is part of the same process (of growing attraction to hardness and dominance), as is (in far more sinister form) the recent rise of far-right political parties even in such moderate and liberal places as Holland, Sweden, and Norway. Men have to toughen up. Men demand it, and women want it, even though they may not approve of the harsh and contemptuous attitude that is part and parcel of the socially demanding process that fosters and then enforces that toughness. Some women don't like losing their baby boys, so they keep them forever. Some women don't like men, and would rather have a submissive mate, even if he is useless. This also provides them with plenty to feel sorry for themselves about, as well. The pleasures of such self-pity should not be underestimated. Men toughen up by pushing themselves, and by pushing each other.

Passages like these show that if Peterson doesn't entirely care for the emergence of these occasionally sinister far-right movements, he certainly sympathizes with elements of their programme. Sometimes the expression of these sympathies comes to the fore through the application of varying standards, as when he is willing to empathize with Heidegger in spite of his Nazism but cannot forgive the bastardization of Marxism decades after Marx's death. But in Chapter Six, it is considerably more subtle. When he is at his worst in *12 Rules for Life*, as across all of Chapter Six, the difference between Peterson and these more dangerous right-wing figures past and present is more a matter of degree than substance. The mass of people must recognize that their life will mostly consist of suffering, and not try to do much to change the social system and its already fragmenting cultural traditions to improve their lot. This will enable the exceptionally few competent people to rise to the top of the natural hierarchy where they belong. The most substantial differences between these past and present right-wing critics and Peterson is that he occasionally flirts with a kind of elitism more akin to Ayn Rand than T.S. Eliot, celebrating the creative superiority and contributions of the capitalist rather than the political sovereign or artist. Peterson also (mostly) decries the use of individual or social violence to maintain the natural hierarchy (though of course, there is an explicit acceptance of state violence to maintain the status quo if necessary). But these differences of degree are likely little consolation to people who are told not to change the social system, even if that would substantially mitigate the suffering that is our unequally shared burden.

Concluding Thoughts on Petersonian Politics

This chapter was necessarily more speculative and interpretive than the earlier chapter on *Maps of Meaning*. This is in part because of the frustratingly imprecise manner by which Peterson expresses his concrete political positions. They are often presented anecdotally, through appeal to highly generalized natural analogies (consider the lobster again), and occasionally by reference to a mish mash of theoretical traditions which often conflict with one another. This makes it very hard to speak about his political positions with any high degree of specificity since they must be drawn out and explicated through interpretation. Peterson enthusiasts may object to such an approach, arguing it doesn't respect the authorial intent since it reads in conclusions to his work which were never explicitly articulated. To that I would give two responses.

The first is that Peterson himself has long acknowledged that interpretation is in some respects 'infinite'. Indeed he even grudgingly conceded in his lectures that post-modern theorists got that right. So even Peterson would concede that authorial intent is not determinative for interpretation once and for all since new positions will still be derived based on a reader's own inclinations, the historical period and most importantly for our purposes the contexts surrounding a piece. My interpretation of Peterson is derived not just from any one given position at any point in *12 Rules for Life* or his papers, but the total mass of comments, lectures and writings gone through for this project. This gives me confidence that the explication given from an 'infinite' sequence of possible interpretations is quite accurate relative to competing ones. My second response is that Peterson himself is in part responsible for the need to explicate his political positions through interpretation because of the lack of precision in his arguments. This belies his calls in Chapter 10 to be 'precise' in one's speech. Peterson is a good stylist most of the time and his prose is clear, but the arguments are not. Clear prose does not necessarily mean analytically 'precise' reasoning; the logician Saul Kripke's arguments in *Naming and Necessity* would be a lot opaquer for many people than a YouTube video by Steven Crowder. That doesn't mean Steven Crowder is more precise in his argumentation than Saul Kripke; he just happens to speak more colloquially. This applies to Peterson's positions. There are a number of points where he argues for a given position, for instance about the naturalness of hierarchy, without engaging in the specific arguments of his opponents. There are other points where Peterson simply asserts various claims, for instance about a discrepancy between sorting one's own life out before trying to sort the world out, where it isn't at all clear that such a divide exists. These ambiguities make it necessary to reconstruct Peterson's positions to try and give them more consistency and precision in order to engage them effectively

These points aside, what is there left to say about Peterson's concrete political positions? I think the *National Review* columnist Nate Hochman put it quite well in his 5 July 2019 column 'The Intellectual Dark Web's Quiet Revolution'. He pointed out that many thoughtful conservative intellectuals, most notably Michael Oakeshott, have opined that a movement to conservatism often begins not because one holds concrete settled convictions but rather because conservatives often drift towards the political right as a 'reaction' to the perceived excesses of the Left. They experience what Hochman calls a 'knee-jerk' reaction which encourages them to look for arguments to rationalize this distaste.

Now of course Hochman's claim is precisely that Peterson and his associates in the Intellectual Dark Web provide a cogent intellectual defence of conservative positions, both constructive and those critical of the Left. To the extent that Peterson's commitment flows from a deeper commitment to a kind of individualism, it is a highly tempered individualism which is very beholden to traditionalism and largely focuses on exercising freedom in private rather than to change anything substantial about the status quo. Petersonian man is a status-minded person focused first and foremost on promotions and raising children, not wishy-washy ideals like actually helping the poor by providing for them or demonstrating that one is worthy of respect through working to establish a political community where the dignity of everyone is treated respectfully. But I think it is easy to hypothesize that Peterson's attraction towards a kind of ordered liberty type conservatism, with the occasional darker undertones bubbling up, was motivated as much by a knee-jerk reaction to the contemporary Left's perceived excesses as any constructive commitments. Many of his constructive political positions, from the necessity of hierarchy to the need for political quietism, are presented as though responding to some perceived radical-Left calls for the elimination of all forms of social structure or the total politicization of all elements of life. To really understand Peterson's politics, we need to look into his disdain for the Left, or at least the so-called 'post-modern neo-Marxists' one hears so much about.

Chapter Four

The Critique of the Left

Comrade Marx, Post-Modern Neo-Marxism and Saint Peterson Part I

'Plato, Rousseau, Fourier, aluminium columns—all that is good only for sparrows, not human society. But since the future form of human society is needed right now, when we're finally ready to take action, in order to forestall any further thought on the subject, I'm proposing my own system of world organization. Here it is!' he said, tapping his notebook. 'I wanted to expatiate on my book to this meeting as briefly as possible, but I see it's necessary to provide a great deal of verbal clarification; therefore my entire explication will take at least ten evenings, corresponding to the number of chapters in my book...' (More laughter was heard) 'Moreover I must declare in advance that my system is not yet complete.' (Laughter again). 'I became lost in my own data and my conclusion contradicts the original premise from which I started. Beginning with unlimited freedom, I end with unlimited despotism. I must add, however, there can be no other solution to the social problem except mine.'
Fyodor Dostoevsky, The Devils

In his great if overlong work *The Devils* Dostoevsky parodies the radical intellectuals and agitators of his day. At a meeting in a small Russian village, the intellectual Shigalyov explains how he has scientifically reached the conclusion, starting from a commitment to 'unlimited freedom', that 90 per cent of the human race must be reduced to eternal servitude for the greater good. Shortly after the erstwhile leader of the group, Peter Stepanovich, son of a past his prime university lecturer, declares that he isn't even interested in violence for the greater good, but for its own sake in order to level everyone down to the same position of uneducated stupidity and impoverishment so they can be easily ruled. Everyone in the society would spy on the other, and violence justified by pieties would be the order of the day.

Dostoevsky, Peterson's favourite author, has received a great deal of praise for effectively predicting the Bolshevik Revolution and the totalitarianism of the Soviet Union decades before either emerged. *The Devils* is his most openly political work, a witheringly black satire of progressive intellectuals and activists that remains funny to this day. At their meeting to discuss revolutionary change, the various leftists squabble about what to call themselves, complain that they are being mislabelled by their peers, reprimand one another for being insufficiently critical of the family and so on. Their personal vulgarities and utter lack of common sense belies their grandiose sense of self-worth and vision for a future where everything will go well so long as they are in charge. Peter Stepanovich is their leader in part because he is more honest with himself, though not with others who are merely pawns to be manipulated. Driven by resentment of his father who ignored him to concentrate on vain personal projects, the nihilistic Stepanovich wants power for its own sake to tyrannize a society which has let him down and is unworthy of any gratitude or reverence. A clever and charismatic figure, he masks his demonic impulses under the guise of egalitarian platitudes and constant calls to arms. Dostoevsky ultimately compares these progressive intellectuals to the swine described in the Gospel of Luke. They became possessed by devils, ran into a lake and were drowned. The Satanic ideas propagated in nineteenth-century Russia led to the destruction of their adherents, and if one follows Peterson, eventually the lives of countless innocents once the Bolsheviks seized power.

I discuss this book at length because I feel it captures the emotional roots of Peterson's own 'knee-jerk' reaction against the

Left. Anyone who spends any time engaging with his writings on left-wing thinking will be struck by how little intellectual rigour Peterson actually applies to analysing it in any good faith. He makes few references to actual texts or authors, and those that appear are often highly skewed or outright wrong. His disdain for leftism seems mainly driven by an immediate distaste for the proposals and aesthetics of 'social justice' activism, understood very broadly, and a deeper conviction that it is driven by some form of resentment and a desire to cause suffering. One can readily point to the injunctions scatted throughout *12 Rules for Life* about 'not blaming capitalism' or that dominance hierarchies are not the fault of 'patriarchy' and so on already cited in the chapter above. But perhaps the most infamous example is his treatment of Marx and Marxism, which seems oriented by the same convictions about motive. More contemporaneously, he seems to have extended this appraisal to the so-called 'post-modern neo-Marxists' of today, whose philosophy apparently guides the utterances of trans and other social justice activists the world over.

My co-authors Conrad Hamilton and Ben Burgis will discuss Peterson's appraisal of Marxism and post-modernism in far more detail in later sections of the book. To avoid redundancy with them, I am not going to focus on these topics at any length. Instead I will simply provide a very brief account of his treatment of these figures and link it to some of his more constructive positions discussed above. I will conclude by showcasing why his most pressing concern, about the efforts to achieve any kind of 'equality of outcome' for all, is misguided.

Comrade Marx, Post-Modern Neo-Marxism and Saint Peterson Part II

Discussing Peterson's treatment of Marxism and post-modern neo-Marxism is even more challenging than analysing his constructive political positions, namely because he has written little about them and these fragments are often very vague. This has of course not stopped him from speaking with great confidence and alarm about the political Left and its alleged theoretical underpinnings. The most substantial pieces of writing on all these theoretical underpinnings appear in Chapter Eleven of *Twelve Rules for Life* under the subheadings 'Postmodernism and the Long Arm of Marx' and 'Lest We Forget: Ideas Have Consequences', amounting to about ten pages. In *Maps of Meaning*, this is about the same amount of space dedicated to just interpreting the story of Marduk in Mesopotamian mythology. The pages include no references to specific works by the authors Peterson claims to understand, so we will once more have to rely on many interpretive inferences to make sense of the morass.

The position staked out in the book isn't substantially different from what is presented in various interviews and lectures, most notably the 2017 interview with the *Epoch Times* and his various addresses. So it would seem that this represents his considered opinion on the subject. Peterson begins by claiming that 'feminist, anti-racist, and queer theories' are 'all heavily influenced by the Marxist humanists'. He then goes on to cite the Frankfurt philosopher Max Horkheimer as an example. This is already a very serious problem, since none of the Frankfurt philosophers promoted humanism, and many were extremely critical of it. This is in part related to their critique of all forms of instrumental reason, predicated on the idea that nature existed to service human needs. Peterson goes on to give a seriously reductive reading of Horkheimer's work, boiling it down to a belief that 'individual freedom or the free market were merely masks that serve to disguise the true conditions of the West, inequality, domination, and exploitation'. This is about as rigorous a reading as saying Peterson believes that uninhibited freedom can only lead to decadence and ultimately a totalitarian impulse; it takes an unbelievable amount of fudging to even begin to make such an assertion. This is a truly frustrating section with no citations, which is very frustrating since even a tertiary reading of *Eclipse of Reason* would show Peterson that he and Horkheimer actually share many of the same concerns. They both fear that excessive scientism has given rise to a nihilistic culture just waiting to embrace fascism. Sadly this bad reading sets the tone for what follows.

The next major figure who gets caricatured is Jacques Derrida, who is now apparently the leader of the post-modernists, whatever that means. Peterson then goes on without citation to claim that Derrida described his 'own ideas as a radicalized form of Marxism'. I must admit that I have never seen Derrida make any such claims. In his 1994 book *Specter's of Marx* Derrida claimed that deconstruction carried on a certain critical and progressive spirit of Marx's. But generally the influence was secondary next to the importance of figures like Saussure, Heidegger, Husserl, Levinas and a host of others. At best Derrida's alleged political and ethical turn in the 1990s constitutes an extended addendum to his important works, most of which were written decades earlier. Peterson then abandons this thread on Derrida to go on extended discussions about the oppression wrought by revolutionary Marxists in the 'Soviet Union, China, Vietnam, Cambodia' and elsewhere. This carries on for about three pages, before we get back to Derrida. On page 310 Peterson makes his famous claim that intellectuals, and particularly French intellectuals, didn't learn from the lessons of Marxist oppression. Instead they transformed Marxist ideas to make them more palatable. It was apparently Derrida who is most responsible for this.

'Derrida, more subtle (than Sartre), substituted the idea of power for the idea of money, and continued on his way. Such linguistic sleight-of-hand gave all the barely repentant Marxists still inhabiting the pinnacles of the West a means to retain their worldview. Society was no longer repression of the poor by the rich.'

Peterson then goes on to claim that Derrida (the great poststructuralist) argued that hierarchical structures emerged to benefit a few and repress the others. He then tries to dally in Derridean linguistics, claiming that Derrida claimed that the binaries established in language were used to exclude the underprivileged. He then goes on to make about the millionth misinterpretation of Derrida's pithy statement that 'there is nothing outside the text' suggesting it means that 'everything is interpretation'. Finally, Peterson claims that it is 'almost impossible to over-estimate the nihilistic and destructive nature of this philosophy'. Ironically his own analysis is living proof that this hyperbolic claim is readily falsifiable. The rest of the section goes on long sermons about how it is competence, not power, that is at the centre of most hierarchies, criticizes gender constructivism (again without citing anyone who holds the views he claims are widespread), criticizes the invocation of group identity as a tool of political mobilization by arguing that such identities can be fractioned right down to the individual (thanks for that) and so on in a rambling sequence that refers to no one while thinking it is taking down everyone. He then concludes that none of this complexity is 'ever discussed by post-modern Marxist thinkers' (odd given they apparently fixate on these issues like the 'North Star') while taking a final paragraph to criticize gender constructivism again, mentions the association between IQ and culture, and throws in a reference to Mao. The point of this is that the alleged efforts of post-modern theorists, apparently led by Derrida, to try to achieve equality of outcome along a variety of different metrics is doomed to end as disastrously as Maoism. Though one might add that they would still constitute a less disastrous intellectual argument than the one presented in these sections of *12 Rules for Life*.

My co-authors Conrad Hamilton and Ben Burgis will elaborate on what is wrong with these interpretations in far more detail later. Needless to say these interpretations are a complete mess, without even any specific references or textual evidence to give a shred of credibility to such an obtuse reading of a complex set of traditions. Peterson apparently thinks that post-modernism is simply Marxism carried on by other means, which both ignores the novelty and underestimates the political quietism of many post-modern theorists. Since only Derrida is referenced it is impossible to know who he is talking about. But simply to clarify quickly, Derrida never claimed that 'everything is interpretation'. He consistently stressed, as far back as his seminal 1966 paper 'Structure, Sign, and Play in the Discourse of the Human Science', that all interpretation of language requires a 'centre', the central sets of interpretations that frame the more idiosyncratic ones.

So while interpretation may be infinite, as Peterson himself would concede, Derrida by no means suggested that this many central interpretations are to be abandoned or what have you. As for Peterson's claims that Derrida developed a binary theory of language oriented around power, where one category of entities dominated over another, I have no idea where he got this idea. Derrida did indeed like to argue that Western philosophy was prone to setting up binaries where one category of entities had been given more ontological and moral weight than another. And indeed some post-modern feminists have used this to criticize cultural emphases on masculinity. But Derrida's point was that these binaries were present in Western thinking since its inception, and the point of deconstruction was merely to draw them to the surface of thought. Moreover he didn't claim that power was at the root of such binary reasoning, which is closer to a Foucaultian claim circa *Madness and Civilization*. And indeed Peterson often seems like he is arguing with Foucault while claiming he is contending with Derrida, all for the purposes of criticizing 'neo-Marxism'. Though if that is the case, he also misses the frequent points where Foucault himself insists that power can be productive, that is will always be present in society, and can ever serve useful purposes. In either case Derrida's claim was that a closer look at the binaries established in Western thought reveals that what seem like opposites are actually highly dependent on one another. To give one example, well explicated in *The Gift of Death,* Derrida claims that we often conceive of living as the opposite of dying. But a closer analysis reveals that many of the actions we take in life are framed by our relationship to death, whether fear, acceptance, denial and so on. So what seems on the surface like a stable binary, with life being more important than death, actually becomes a more dynamic relationship when deconstructed.

The remainder of Peterson's comments are about such a scattered array of topics they needn't be analysed in much detail. Needless to say he mashes together a number of positions such as Marxist materialism, social constructivism, gender performativity theory, Maoism and so on that are very different and which any serious scholar would treat with considerable care. But as discussed in Chapter Three, most often Peterson gets involved in politics or political-theoretical approaches, any concern with a modicum of specificity gets thrown out of the window. Everything becomes determined by idealized highly general categories without care. This could be readily dismissed if it wasn't for his influence on the centre and the Right. My suspicion is that many people buy into his simplistic narratives about the Left because they sound vaguely plausible. There are a few scattered references to major authors the public often associates with the Left, a couple of clear and strident quotations from Orwell and Solzhenitsyn, and sufficiently clunky intellectual sounding neologisms like 'post-modern neo-Marxism' or 'cultural Marxism'. But none of Peterson's analysis is actually done with any care or knowledge of what he is talking about. He would be well advised to adapt Rule Six into 'set your understanding in basic order before you criticize 150 years of critical theory'.

Chapter Five

Conclusion

The Reactionary Impulse and Post-Modernity

It should come as little surprise that someone like Jordan Peterson made it big. In some respects we might go full Jung and say there was a certain inevitability about it. For decades a certain style of left-wing activism has dominated the cultural perception of the Left, particularly in right-wing media like Breitbart and the Daily Wire. Concern about social justice warriors, free speech activism, political correctness and so on dominate the headlines of these and other outlets. Peterson's own attacks on Bill C-16, social justice activism and so-called post-modern neo-Marxism hit the zeitgeist perfectly. Moreover, he had a unique selling point in being a tenured academic at a respectable university whose research was broadly in the humanities, while also dipping into more scientific territory at points. This gave him the kind of authority figures like Dave Rubin and even Ben Shapiro can only emulate, which was a substantial advantage when appealing to conservatives who claim to despise academics while also craving intellectual validation.

But Peterson's appeal cannot simply be chalked up to circumstances in transient political culture. Certainly he knew how to manipulate circumstances skilfully and strategically, whether through well formulated pithy statements and smart sounding neologisms or a well-designed website. Yet still, there is more going on than appears beneath the eye. Since the 1980s neoliberal forms of capitalism and governance have been sweeping the globe. These have had a corrosive impact on traditional cultures and practices; sweeping away rural communities in the face of urbanization, bringing in huge swathes of cheap migrant labour from far away countries, and transforming local environments into unrecognizable idols to economic 'efficiency'. At the same time inequality has been escalating quickly, coupled with a growing precarity in employment and quality of life. Real wages have stagnated or shrunk for many individuals over the neoliberal decades. We also witnessed the transparent ownership of the political class by capital in the 2008 recession, which exacerbated many of the aforementioned problems as billions were given to the finance sector. Finally, technological changes in communication and media have transformed the way we interact with and frame political counterparts. As Neil Postman put it in his great book *Amusing Ourselves to Death,* many of these new media rewarded simplistic narratives based on antagonistic binaries.

All these developments characterize neoliberal societies governed by post-modern cultures in the early twenty-first century. It is an uncertain time, and it should come as no surprise that a certain kind of post-modern conservatism would emerge. These post-modern conservatives are deeply sensitive to the identities they associate with being dissolved, and deal with strong feelings of anxiety and even resentment which drive them to ever more reactionary positions. Given this, someone like Peterson will naturally be very attractive to many. He provides a seemingly total framework through which to make sense of an increasingly unmoored world. Moreover Peterson also presents a tidy narrative which, if unfair to the subtleties of his work at its best, also is very appealing to many post-modern conservatives. He acknowledges that their traditional identities have come under immense threat from the dynamics of (post) modernization. And Peterson goes a step further and claims that the primary individuals responsible are post-modern neo-Marxists, feminists, LGBTQ activists and so on. While his account is undeniably more sophisticated than the reductive narratives put forward by someone like Ben Shapiro, this is itself part of the appeal. A pedigreed academic like Peterson can vindicate the unconscious suppositions and prejudices of post-modern conservatives by arguing that their antagonisms have a legitimate intellectual and moral basis.

This in turn can make it very difficult for leftists to actually contend against Peterson. Many have attempted to bring him down through accusations of sexism, racism, transphobia and so on. While there may be some truth to any and even all of these claims, in the eyes of Peterson's followers they only serve to reinforce the antagonistic narrative they were already primed to believe and which the good doctor has legitimated a million times over. To their minds, it proves that a cabal of social justice oriented post-modernists are trying to attack him using all the predictable tools in their arsenal. Since Peterson's followers have been primed to regard these kinds of attacks as illegitimate and biased, deploying them in all but the most transparent cases will be as useful as punching a brick wall. If anything it may only affirm everything that he has claimed.

The more effective way to combat Peterson is to understand both his thinking and what he represents. In other words there are things the Left can learn from Jordan Peterson, and we had best get in the business of learning them.

What Can the Left Take Away from Jordan Peterson?

The main point the Left can take away from Jordan Peterson is that a politics of antagonism needs to be linked to a more constructive and meaningful political viewpoint. In Peterson's case much of the latter is implicit and often highly ambiguous. But it does not matter since many of his followers recognize elements of his politics and empathize with them. They find resonance not just in his insistence that post-modern neo-Marxists are destroying Western civilization. His followers also gravitate towards the emphasis on tradition, his appeals to religious tropes which many thought were outdated, and even his tough love insistence that a person can improve their lot through hard work and determination. Coupled to this is Peterson's insistence that achieving success under difficult conditions demonstrates a kind of superiority which justifies one's place in the social hierarchy, and even purifies and beatifies one's soul by providing an answer to existential quandaries. This is an inspiring vision to many reactionaries living within post-modern cultures, especially those belonging to historically privileged social groups who want a justification for their position. And of course a contrasting justification for why those lower on the social totem pole are where they are.

The Left is widely seen as not having a similarly constructive vision of the world. As the Marxist David Harvey would put it, many people see the contemporary Left as driven by various forms of 'militant particularism' which agitate for the inclusion of previously marginalized groups into the political status quo. These are obviously necessary movements, and the story of gaining rights for women, LGBTQ races and racial minorities is an inspiring one that needs to be continued. But it also lacks some of the big picture emphasis on justice, good, evil and so on that is replete in Peterson's work. While such big pictures are often simplistic, and Peterson's certainly can be, they are also often inspiring. They also allow people to define their political identity not just by what they oppose, but what they are for. If the Left is to combat Peterson, it needs to generate widespread enthusiasm for a systematic alternative to the status quo that is both radical enough to warrant moral fidelity and realistic enough that individuals can put their faith in achieving it. Programmes like Ocasio Cortez's Green New Deal, with its ambitions to combat both climate change and mass poverty, and politicians like Bernie Sanders and Pedro Sanchez are on the right track. Following Mike Watson in *Can the Left Learn to Meme?* and Contrapoints, we can also point out that a renewed emphasis on political aesthetics is necessary. Figures like Peterson and Ben Shapiro are appealing in part because they give off a veneer of sophistication while providing a great deal of information in an accessible and entertaining fashion that engages their audience at several different levels. They complement that with a variety of media to continuously interact with their audience and provide new content. The Left can learn these tactics and approaches from people like Peterson and use them to advance a more inspiring and plausible vision of the future oriented around progressive principles rather than reactionary impulses. If it does not, the Lobster King and his beta-crustaceans may wind up having the last laugh.

Part II

Peterson's Reckoning with the Left:
By Conrad Hamilton

Introduction

The obvious question that will arise, as regards this text, is: why do it? Why co-author a book on Jordan Peterson?

The first answer is straightforward. Peterson, while not a *philosopher* of titanic significance, is an academic. In this sense, his ideas warrant rigorous response. He is also an important figure to the Right—indeed, it would be far more accurate to describe Peterson as the leader of the 'Intellectual Dark Web' than to describe Derrida, as Peterson does, as the 'leader of the postmodernists'. Whatever his defects, Peterson represents an undeniable upgrade in this respect from previous models such as Milo Yiannopoulos. Who knows? Maybe one day the alt-right will get its Heidegger.

The second answer is slightly more complex. When I was first offered the opportunity to write about Peterson, I hesitated. At the time, I worried that the publication of a book such as this one would have the inadvertent consequence of legitimating his ideas (if you'll pardon the arrogance implicit in the assumption that my commentary could have a *legitimating effect*!). Certainly, Peterson's popularity owes a great deal to the attention that's been given to him by what's commonly described as the 'Left'. Adherents of politically-correct, 'callout culture' have, in particular—and this is a matter of record—played an important role in advancing his agenda, with the ersatz outrage that accompanies many of his public statements doubtlessly helping to engender the impression that he *must be important*. Upon reflection, however, it occurred to me that—given his vast popularity, and the millions of books he's sold—Peterson has *already* entrenched himself in the public imagination to a degree that does not allow ignoring him to be a viable strategy. I would not have agreed to write this text a year ago. But it is perhaps symptomatic of our extremely perilous political state that, now, direct engagement seems to me to be the best option.

None of this, of course, should be taken as tantamount to the suggestion that this book could somehow suffice to reverse the success of Peterson himself, let alone the political energies that he staked his fame upon. For that, a far more general mobilization—both theoretical and practical—would be required; one committed to addressing the social fissures his work exploits rather than merely lobbing allegations of racism or sexism at him. To such an initiative, all I can offer is this modest contribution. Peterson has spoken at length about the risks posed by 'compelled speech'. Here's mine.

Believe me,

dear reader,

Your devoted,

Conrad Bongard Hamilton

22 August 2019

Chapter Six

Peterson's Showbiz Roots, OR from the Lecture Hall to Hollywood

People often look back at their lives and they say: well, you know, I got knocked out of my little paradise by, you know, this particular event. But, looking back, it really made me grow up, it really made me mature.

Jordan Peterson, What Matters

The Unbearable Heaviness of Being Peterson

And then, in an instant, Peterson was everywhere. DESTROYING a swath of 'crazy feminist' interlocutors with FACTS and LOGIC, snuggling up on a sofa with the factually challenged hosts of *Fox & Friends*, sermonizing from *12 Rules for Life* on his seemingly never-ending book tour, and even sparring onstage with Marxist luminary/stand-up comedian Slavoj Žižek — since the latter part of 2016, Peterson has been virtually unescapable (and the word 'virtual' is used here deliberately, given the particular currency of his thought in the digital sphere). Yet while Peterson has quickly ascended to the status of being the intellectual standard-bearer of the political right — a distinction that he's testy about, having repeatedly described himself as a classical liberal with limited interest in race or nation qua collective — few have posed the question: just where does the Jordan Peterson phenom *come from*?

There is, of course, Peterson's own origin story, one that appears prominently in his first book, 1999's *Maps of Meaning: The Architecture of Belief*: that of a man who grew up in the intellectually unpromising environs of northern Alberta, and even dallied with democratic socialism before a series of cataclysmic dreams of atomic war led him to an awareness of the capacity of humans for evil, and thus of the perils of collectivist ideology (the basis for his later confrontation with the politically-correct culture of academia). However, we should be careful of rehashing this narrative for two reasons. First, because it's romanticized to a degree that makes one suspect that taking it at face value would be roughly equivalent to watching a long cut of *Purple Rain* and assuming it's a literal account of Prince's musical apprenticeship. Second, because Peterson's self-supplied backstory in *Maps of Meaning*, while characterized by his signature near-limitless self-belief, in fact *presages* the moment where he would have the opportunity to shift the culture by roughly 20 years. Indeed, for that, Peterson would have to wait until September 2016 — when the crisis surrounding Bill C-16 catapulted him to the forefront of Canadian national consciousness.

The particulars of Peterson's intellectual biography, then, do little to illuminate or help us understand the socio-political conjuncture that, in 2016, would elevate him to being the thinker *par excellence* of the reactionary set. Nor can they show us just how calculatedly Peterson went about gauging the political changes afoot and seeking to reorient his career on the basis of them. In 1999, *Maps of Meaning* did not have much of an impact for a couple of reasons. The first of these is because it's a dense academic tome that never bothers to translate its intellectual contrarianism into a register that would allow it to be appreciated by a mass audience — which makes sense, given how comparatively remote from quotidian existence the culture wars of the late nineties were compared to in 2018, when *12 Rules for Life: An Antidote to Chaos* was published. The second is because it's simply *not a very good book*, with Peterson's effort to ground Jungian archetypes in neurobiology being a task that even a more competent academic would struggle with, as if one had sought to prove the truth of Heidegger by looking at neuroimages of individuals with anxiety disorders. This tendency — an overreliance on scientific data coupled with a penchant for grossly exaggerating the extent to which it supports more conjectural claims—is, to be sure, vintage Peterson. But even foreknowledge of Peterson's vocabulary of rhetorical manoeuvres does little to diminish how galling it is to see him shift from a comparatively benign discussion of neuropsychology into the claim that it affirms Jung's theory of archetypes in the space of just a few pages (or, sometimes, the same paragraph). Thus readers of the text are confronted with seemingly unremarkable passages such as these:

Empirical (classical) 'objects' are either one thing or another. Nature, by contrast—the great unknown—is one thing and its (affective) opposite at the same time, and in the same place. The novel, primeval experience was (and remains) much too complex to be gripped, initially, by rational understanding, as understood in the present day. Mythic imagination, 'willing' to sacrifice discriminatory clarity for inclusive phenomenological accuracy, provided the necessary developmental bridge.

Myth, Mayhem and Biology

Okay, so far so good—myths arise due to what Peterson explains, appealing to neurobiology, as 'the need for overlay of familiarity granted by shared frameworks of action and interpretation'. But then Peterson continues: 'The earliest embodiments of nature are therefore symbolic combinations of rationally irreconcilable attributes; monsters, essentially feminine, who represent animal and human, creation and destruction, birth and cessation of experience.'

Wait, wait—run that one by me again. So the need for 'inclusive phenomenological accuracy' that guides myths justifies Jung's association of femininity with the 'irrational' unconscious? But then, as Peterson helpfully elaborates elsewhere in the same chapter:

Femininity shares emotional valence with novelty and threat, furthering the utility of the female as metaphoric grist, because of the union that exists within experience between creation of one thing, and destruction and transformation of another. The processes of embryogenesis itself require that blood change form, as the fetus thrives on the 'blood' of its mother. The act of birth itself is traumatic, painful, dangerous and frightening, recapitulating the natural theme of creation, transformation and destruction.

So basically, nature is personified as a feminine monstrosity because women's biological processes are terrifying (also because 'Every individual's primordial world experience is experience of mother, who is the world itself, in initial developmental stages'). Yet what's interesting is that, in his zeal to yoke together scientific claims with the vagaries of psychoanalytic logic, Peterson doesn't even bother to seriously consult the anthropological record to confirm the veracity of his arguments. As Paul Thagard has observed, for instance, Peterson's assertion that all myths conform to the triune structure of Father/Mother/Son is simply not true (Thagard cites Iroquois and Chinese mythologies as not being in conformance with this structure)—something Peterson glosses over by focusing on Mesopotamian and Judeo-Christian mythology at the expense of other traditions (and sprinkling in a few brief comments on Buddhism for good measure)[1]. To this observation we might add that Peterson's view of the feminine as *a priori* associable with monstrous irrationality seems to belie a similar overdependence on the written records furnished by these self-same traditions. For since the nineteenth century—the lineage running from Bachofen to Morgan to Engels—it has been often claimed that much of the written material that had been hitherto assumed to be reflective of humanity *tout court* is more limited in its purview than was previously imagined. Indeed, in Morgan's seminal 1877 work *Ancient Society*, Morgan, supplied with extensive data from US government-sponsored fieldwork, puts forth the view that that the system of matrilineal descent characteristic of Iroquois gentes (clans) was the system of decent that prevailed across much of the world prior to the extensive development of agriculture (in particular, the acquisition of cattle by men, who by trading it with their future bride's kinsfolk were able to achieve a shift to patrilocal residence). If one accepts this, it follows that—in so far as developed writing systems did not appear until *after* the dawn of agriculture —many of the myths Peterson takes as emerging from the structure of the human mind in fact have a more specific, patriarchal heritage. In terms of erudition, this would make Peterson about the theoretical equivalent of Tony Soprano declaring that the Chinese could not have invented spaghetti due to the fact that people who eat with sticks would not have created something you need a fork to eat.

Of course, Morgan's thesis of primordial matrilineality has been deeply controversial since its inception. Indeed, for the bulk of the twentieth century, A.R. Radcliffe's 1924 work 'The Mother's Brother in South Africa'—an essay which sought to cast Henri Junod's description of the residual matrilineal aspects of the Thonga of Mozambique as mere 'extensions of sentiment' that had no bearing on its historical kinship structure—was taken as the last word on this controversy. But more recently, the discovery of genetic data on sub-Saharan African hunter-gatherers that indicates a long-term historical preference for matrilocal residence, as well the thorough discreditation of George Murdocl's 1967 *Ethnographic Atlas* by University of Utah anthropologist Helen Alvarez, have done a great deal to renew the credibility of the Bachofen-Morgan-Engels tradition.

The hypothesis that the majority of pre-agricultural societies were *matrilineal*, and thus were not inclined to personify the feminine as 'monstrous' in the fashion described by Peterson, should not, it should be said, be taken as tantamount to the claim that these societies were *matriarchal*. For while Johann Jakob

115

Bachofen asserts this in his 1861 text *Das Mutterrecht* [*Mother Right*]—a text that's arguments are supported by meticulously compiled citations from ancient literature rather than from field studies—subsequent thinkers influenced by his work such as Lewis Henry Morgan and Friedrich Engels took exception to Bachofen's conflation of matrilineality with matriarchy. According to Morgan and Engels, Bachofen had been correct in his claim that there existed a pre-monogamanian state in which relative sexual permissiveness prevailed, and in which lineage was traced maternally (a state that Morgan—and in turn, Engels—identifies with the organization into gentes and the punaluan family structure). But to describe this pre-monogamian dispensation as 'matriarchal' is a misnomer for the simple reason that there did not exist, prior to the appropriation of agricultural surpluses by men and the advent of private wealth, a basis for the social domination of one sex by another. What can be found, then, in most gentile societies are comparatively slight variances in gendered social power coupled with structures that suggest primordial matrilineality—which is logical, since absent monogamy and the social control of women's sexuality it is exceedingly difficult to trace lineage through the paternal line (since DNA paternity tests didn't exist in the ancient world).

The question of the anthropological development of human societies has immense implications for the study of mythology. For the myths that Peterson takes as universal are, seen from this paradigm, myths that have been passed down in writing from societies that had already imposed patriarchal dominance—and, consequently, are prone to portraying the feminine as alternatively repulsive and seductive, inexorable and otherly. This is true of Aeschylus' *Oresteia*, a text that Bachofen interpreted as an allegory for the replacement of father right by mother right in Heroic Age Greece. It's also true of *The Odyssey*, which finds Odysseus hobnobbing with —and even being held as a sex slave by—goddesses on the lam in the Mediterranean

Sea from a Greek pantheon that had been male-dominated since the castration of Uranus by Cronus or earlier. It is even, Peterson will be shattered to discover given his impassioned lectures on it, true of *The Lion King* ('the sunrise is an allegory for the dawn of consciousness', 'the day is a journey, like the French *journée'²*), in which an effete gay lion (Scar) conspires unsuccessfully to rob the King's masculine heir (Simba) of his royal birth right.

Peterson's Primordial Patriarchy

Of course, given the significant anthropological debates that continue to prevail over the kinship structures of societies that lacked developed writing systems, one should be careful about being too matter-of-fact in their descriptions of them. But what *is* clear is that these controversies in the field pose a significant obstacle to Peterson's clumsy efforts to map Jungian metaphysics onto neurobiology. In an effort to redress this oversight, Peterson—years later, in *12 Rules for Life*—musters a brief critique of Bachofen and those influenced by his works. Given that much of the integrity of *Maps of Meaning* hinges on this question, one might imagine that he would make a thorough effort to explore the question of patrilineality versus matrilineality in early human history, in an effort to set his life's work on a firmer footing. But this *is* Peterson, so instead we get what could be described as the typical recipe: a dismissal of the weakest expressions of the matrilineality hypothesis available (Bachofen's original speculative anthropology and feminist theology), a few citations from Jung and his followers, and *voilà*:

> The feminine, as a whole, is unknown nature outside the bounds of culture, creation and destruction: she is the protective arms of mother and the destructive element of time, the beautiful virgin-mother and the swamp-dwelling hag. This archetypal entity was confused with an objective, historical reality, back in the late 1800s, by a Swiss

anthropologist named Johann Jakob Bachofen. Bachofen proposed that humanity had passed through a series of developmental stages in its history.

The first, roughly speaking (after a somewhat anarchic and chaotic beginning), was Das Mutterrecht—a society where women held the dominant positions of power, respect and honour, where polyamory and promiscuity ruled, and where any certainty of paternity was absent. The second, the Dionysian, was a phase of transition, during which these original matriarchal foundations were overturned and power was taken by men. The third phase, the Apollonian, still reigns today. The patriarchy rules, and each woman belongs exclusively to one man.

Bachofen's ideas became profoundly influential, in certain circles, despite the absence of any historical evidence to support them. One Marija Gimbutas, for example—an archaeologist—famously claimed in the 1980s and 1990s that a peaceful goddess-and-woman-centred culture once characterized Neolithic Europe. She claimed that it was supplanted and suppressed by an invasive hierarchical warrior culture, which laid the basis for modern society. Art historian Merlin Stone made the same argument in his book *When God Was a Woman*.

And then:

Carl Jung had encountered Bachofen's ideas of primordial matriarchy decades earlier. Jung soon realized, however, that the developmental progression described by the earlier Swiss thinker represented a psychological rather than a historical reality. He saw in Bachofen's thought the same processes of projection of imaginative fantasy on to the external world that had led to the population of the cosmos with constellations and gods...for Jung, consciousness...is constantly tempted to sink back down into dependency and unconsciousness, and to shed its existential burden. It is aided in that pathological desire by anything that opposes enlightenment, articulation, rationality, self-determination, strength and competence — by anything that shelters too much, and therefore smothers and devours. Such overprotection is Freud's Oedipal familial nightmare, which we are rapidly transforming into social policy.

And then we're off, into a commentary on the figure of the 'Terrible Mother' in *The Little Mermaid* followed by a reprisal of the chapter's main thesis, decrying the feminization of society (and young men in particular). Nowhere does Peterson address the large number of concrete examples of societies that were or are matrilineal or matrilocal, from the !Kung peoples to the Navajo (if Peterson wants an example more up his alley, he could've even tackled ancient Minoan Crete). Nor does he discuss the works of Lewis Henry Morgan, let alone that of subsequent cultural anthropologists who attempted and often succeeded in challenging the notion of universal patriarchy, from Margaret Mead to Helen Alvarez. The title of this chapter (or 'rule', if you will), by the way: 'Do Not Bother Children When They Are Skateboarding'. This represents a rare concession to gender-neutral language by Peterson: in fact, in his experience, these 'amazing' kids are 'almost always boys'.

Maps of Public Funding

Maps of Meaning does not appear to have been, by all available metrics, taken too seriously as an academic text. Not any more than a book featuring 15 (!) pictures of the Tolkienesque 'Dragon of Chaos' sandwiched into various unnecessary visual illustrations throughout its duration could have been expected to, anyway. Indeed, the only published review of it that Google turns up prior to 2016 comes from Safa Alai — a Google employee and self-described proponent of 'nature mysticism' who actually chides Peterson for the 'plethora of assumptions' he makes about religious figures such as Christ or Buddha 'despite not having met' them. But it did represent a crucial pivot in Peterson's career. For just as he had been readying *Maps of Meaning* for publication, in 1998, Peterson took up a post as full professor at the University of Toronto—a downgrade from Harvard, where he'd served as an assistant and associate professor, but still Canada's largest and arguably best university. From there, Peterson would endeavour upon his own version of the cycle of death and rebirth he's so wont to talk about, swapping academic obscurity for the courtship of a popular audience.

Crucial to this sagacious step in Peterson's heroic journey was the existence, so it goes, of publicly-funded educational programming in Toronto. In 2004, one year before the launch of YouTube, tvo (TVOntario) aired a 13-episode series of Peterson's lectures centring on *Maps of Meaning*. Why exactly tvo chose to devote this much airtime to an academic hardly considered a titanic figure in his field is difficult to say. Though in his foreword to *12 Rules for Life*, fellow University of Toronto faculty member Norman Doidge sheds some light on the attributes that attracted tvo producer and 'Polish émigré' Wodek Szemberg to Peterson:

Wodek is a silver-haired, lion-maned hunter, always on the lookout for potential public intellectuals, who knows how to spot people who can *really* talk in front of a TV camera and who look authentic because they are (the camera picks up on that). He often invites such people to these salons. That day Wodek brought a psychology professor, from my own University of Toronto, who fit the bill: intellect and emotion in tandem. Wodek was the first to put Jordan Peterson in front of a camera, and thought of him as a teacher in search of students—because he was always ready to explain. And it helped that he liked the camera and that the camera liked him back.

Doidge's forward is frequently ridiculous—in it, he describes Peterson as a 'cowboy psychologist' of a type whose sensibilities have been honed by long periods spent outside in 'the harsh elements'. He also, in an early effort to shield Peterson from charges of chauvinism, characterizes him as 'tormented by what happened in Europe to the Jews' to a degree he's never seen in someone 'born Christian' of his generation, and as being especially endowed with the 'good will and courage' to combat 'right-wing bigotry'.[3] Yet while Doidge's hagiographic flourishes are, how shall we say, dubitable, his foreword nevertheless offers us insight into the way that Peterson's uniquely telegenic charisma played a role in permitting him, in the mid-2000s, to make his first foray into public intellectualism. With, it would seem, further help from Szemberg—an in-house producer at tvo—Peterson would successfully parlay his lecture series into additional PR opportunities, including dozens of appearances on the network flagship current affairs television programme *The Agenda with Steve Paikin*, in which Paikin does a generally impeccable job of looking bewildered as Peterson makes comments that range from prejudicial ('women have higher levels of negative emotion than men') to bizarre ('The reason [*Avatar* is] propaganda is because it presents things in a terribly one-sided manner...so nature is perfect; culture and the military is absolutely evil...Cameron seems to have absolutely no gratitude to technology').[4]

This interest in penetrating popular discourse, as Doidge seems to imply, carried over into *12 Rules for Life*, which in large part appears to be an effort to translate Peterson's scholarly bona fides into a book that's consumable by a mass audience. In the text's 'Overture', for instance, which follows immediately on the heels of Doidge's prelim, Peterson explains how *12 Rules*

for Life's conceit—to supply individuals with a set of injunctions
regarding how to better their lives—derived, in all seriousness,
from a systematic gauging of which of his Quora posts received
the most views and upvotes:

> Soon after, I answered another question: 'What are the
> most valuable things everyone should know?' I wrote a list
> of rules, or maxims; some dead serious, some tongue-in-
> cheek—'Be grateful in spite of your suffering,' 'Do not do
> things that you hate,' 'Do not hide things in the fog,' and so
> on. The Quora readers appeared pleased with this list. They
> commented on and shared it. They said such things as 'I'm
> definitely printing this list out and keeping it as a reference.
> Simply phenomenal,' and 'You win Quora. We can just close
> the site now.' Students at the University of Toronto, where I
> teach, came up to me and told me how much they liked it. To
> date, my answer to 'What are the most valuable things ...' has
> been viewed by 120,000 people and been upvoted 2300 times.
> Only a few hundred of the roughly six hundred thousand
> questions on Quora have cracked the two-thousand-upvote
> barrier. My procrastination-induced musings hit a nerve. I
> had written a 99.9 percentile answer.

A hallelujah moment, then, for Peterson, in which a decidedly
non-99.9 percentile professor discovers he's capable of making
posts on Quora that earn that self-same level of online approval.
Later, as Peterson explains, after being contacted by a literary
agent impressed with his appearance on a radio show for
Canada's national broadcaster, titled *Just Say No To Happiness*, he
went to work on a book that was intended to reprise and further
develop the 40 'rules for life' he'd originally written for Quora
(an endeavour he characterizes as his second attempt to write
a book with broad appeal, after an aborted effort to produce a
'more accessible version' of *Maps of Meaning*). Somewhere along

the line, the number of rules in the book was cut to 'twenty-five and then to sixteen and then finally, to the current twelve' — less than the original 40, to be sure, but still two more than Moses, whom Doidge compares Peterson to in the text's foreword ('People don't clamor for rules, even in the Bible...when Moses comes down the mountain').

En route to publication, *12 Rules for Life* went through, by Peterson's own admission, an assiduous editorial process. This involved both his official editor as well as former student Gregg Hurwitz, whose credentials for editing a philosophy book appear to have consisted solely of having authored a 2016 thriller, *Orphan X*, about — according to Wikipedia — a programme that 'train[s] orphans so they can be assassins for government agencies' (Bradley Cooper is slated to produce and star in an upcoming film adaptation). Not that it mattered: Hurwitz, by surreptitiously inserting rules from Peterson's Quora list into a burgeoningly successful trilogy of potboilers[5], had already beaten Peterson to the punch in bringing his Internet edicts to the masses, thereby affirming his former professor's 'supposition of their attractiveness'. Equally worth noting is the long duration the book required to edit: 3 years. For given the myriad misreadings that permeate *12 Rules for Life* — including, perhaps most egregiously, that of French poststructuralist philosopher Jacques Derrida, whose ideas Peterson is unable to separate from either those of Marx or Foucault — it is worth posing the question: just what did his editors spend 3 years doing?

The Birth of Controversy

Well, tailoring it to the tastes of Peterson's new-fangled audience, for one. In autumn 2016 while *12 Rules for Life* was in the throes of being edited — and really, it's impossible to address the book's context without discussing this — Peterson experienced a supernova of media and Internet interest, due to the controversy surrounding Bill C-16 in Canada. This is not to say that he had not already made inroads online: an already academic adopter of YouTube, the public lectures Peterson placed on the platform received over a million views by April 2016. His intervention in the debate over the usage of gendered pronouns, however, carried him to a whole other level of intellectual celebrity. By the time Penguin Random House Canada published *12 Rules for Life* a year-and-a-half later, in January 2018, the videos on Peterson's YouTube channel had received over 100 million views. Once described by one of his interlocutors on The Agenda as having views that resemble a '1974 issue of Cosmopolitan' magazine, Peterson had become, in the short span of 18 months, the world's biggest public intellectual.

The controversy that unfurled at the University of Toronto—and in the broader Canadian and, ultimately, global media—requires a little bit of unpacking to fully understand. On 27 September 2019, Peterson uploaded a video to his YouTube channel titled 'Part I: Fear and Law' or—alternatively, since one title simply wouldn't suffice—'Professor against political correctness: Part I.' The impetus for this video was, as he would divulge to the *National Post* around the same time it was published, a memo he received from the HR department at the University of Toronto outlining new mandatory anti-racist and anti-bias training. 'That disturbs me because if someone asked me to take anti-bias training, I think I am agreeing that I am sufficiently racist or biased to need training,' Peterson scoffed to the *National Post*—a bizarre quote, since he would later state while on *The Agenda* that he was personally never obligated to take the training, restricted as it was to HR personnel. In the video, however, Peterson mentions this memo only passingly. Instead, the bulk of its contents are devoted to criticizing Bill C-16, a law introduced to the Canadian House of Commons in May 2016 that proposed adding gender expression and gender identity as protected grounds to the Canadian Human Rights Act, and also to certain Criminal Code provisions (when Peterson made the video, Bill C-16 was in the process of acquiring legislative approval; it received royal assent on 19 June 2017).

In many respects, 'Professor against political correctness' serves as a trial balloon for the transitioning of Peterson's image from that of a mildly risqué psychology lecturer to that of a free speech martyr for hire. His language, for instance, is sometimes more cautious; more equivocal, than in later public appearances—understandably so, since he'd yet to build himself up into a brand capable of generating revenue independent of the university system. But for all this, his vitriol is still palpable, and 'Professor against political correctness' finds him in, what would've, up to that point, seemed like rare form. No less than three times in the video, he claims that the Canadian Human Rights Act has become so draconian that he or others could potentially go to 'jail' for failing to comply with its diktats: 'I don't recognize another person's right to determine what pronouns I used to address them. I won't do it…it's the sort of thing I'm going to question, and if someone should be put in jail for questioning that, then I guess I should be put in jail.' He indulges in his logical fallacy of choice, a version of the ontological argument in which the mere existence of ubiquitous social norms are proof of their inevitability: 'if you ran a correlation analysis between gender identity and sexual orientation, the correlation is going to be something like .95, which indicates almost perfect correlation for the vast majority of people'. He even accuses the sitting premier, Liberal Kathleen Wynne, of a gay Mafioso-style conspiracy: 'Social justice warrior type activists are over-represented in the current provincial government…I can't help but manifest the suspicion that that's partly because our current Premier is lesbian in her sexual preference.'

For all of his histrionic protestations of his unwillingness to be complicit in the perpetuation of 'murderous' left-wing ideology, it should be noted here that, in 'Professor against political correctness', Peterson mischaracterizes the impacts of Bill C-16 in several ways. For one, he doesn't adequately differentiate between the Canadian Human Rights Act and the law that applies to the province he resides in, the Ontario Human Rights Code. For while the former applies to federally regulated activities, the latter applies to provincially regulated ones—including universities. What this means, in effect, is that Peterson had *already* been subject to legislation barring discrimination based on gender identity in his workplace since 2012, when Ontario became the first province to adopt said provisions into its human rights code (Ontario's premier at the time this legislation was passed was, like Peterson, a straight, white male, albeit just the second Roman-Catholic to hold the premiership—Dalton McGuinty). Additionally, it's highly unlikely that misgendering his students would've constituted hate speech under either provincial or federal law. As professor of law at the University of Toronto Brenda Cossman would later state to *Torontoist* 3 months after the controversy first broke out: 'I don't think there's any legal expert that would say that [this] would meet the threshold for hate speech in Canada… If he advocated genocide against trans people, he would be in violation, but misusing pronouns is not what that provision of the code is about.' *Finally*, even if Peterson *was* successfully brought in front of the Ontario Human Rights Commission due to the content of his courses, it's impossible that he would ever face jail time, due to the fact his offence would be deigned illegal rather than criminal (the means at the disposal of the OHRC to enforce the provincial human rights code include levying fines, demanding behavioural correction and forcing people to undergo training).

To point out the distortions and fallacies embraced by Peterson in his tirade against Bill C-16 and human rights legislation more generally should not be taken as tantamount to the claim that there haven't been instances of abuse that have occurred in the past with its enforcement. Rather, it's to illustrate that, even when faced with what should've been, by all accounts, an easy opportunity to go after the excesses of a human rights enforcement structure, that—as of this being written—is being wielded by a xenophobic pre-op trans woman to try to compel immigrant women to wax her genitals, Peterson *still* manages to miss the mark, drawing comparisons with Nazi Germany and the Soviet Union and generally showing a lack of basic literacy about the subject in question. Given this, it's quite possible that—had the right-wing media not mobilized itself to paint Peterson as a lone man selflessly pitting himself against a sea of politically-correct apparatchiks bent on the suspension of free speech rights *tout court*—this scandal would've simply fizzled out.

But alas, no. On 28 September 2016—one day after Peterson published 'Professor against political correctness: Part I' on YouTube—Canada's right-leaning National Post sprang into action. The article in question, 'U of T professor attacks political correctness, says he refuses to use genderless pronouns' is about what one would describe from the outlet, subtly privileging Peterson's viewpoint while offering comment from a few parties at the University of Toronto critical of him (and failing to point out the falsehoods upon which Peterson's protest was premised—though at least we get to see our hero hilariously ID'd as 'Peterson, a white male in his mid-50s'). The following day, BuzzFeed decided to scramble the jets and get offended, issuing an article, 'A Toronto Professor Is Facing Criticism For Saying He Won't Recognize Gender-Neutral Identities [sic]', explicitly structured to convey the views of Peterson's on-campus opponents. The National Post and BuzzFeed thereby succeeded in implementing the first two steps in what has since become a wholly reliable three-step waltz: conservative party offers more or less qualified praise for Peterson; liberal/SJW outlet vociferously responds, offering their own take; Peterson gains in visibility and furthers his career (and now, *voilà*, this book).

The National Post's fairly innocuous 28 September article was just a prelude, however. For as the scandal deepened over the course of the next month, with Peterson being the recipient of two letters from the University of Toronto's administration and faculty forcefully reminding him of his obligations to comply with applicable human rights law (something Peterson responded to by disdainfully dissecting the letters on YouTube for his rapidly-growing following), an all-star roster of some of the *National Post*'s most esteemed writers began to jostle for who could heap the most hyperbole on the embattled professor. The *National Post* had its own agenda, of course: human rights enforcement agencies in Canada had long been the newspaper's *bête noire*. Indeed, one of their regular columnists, Mark Steyn, had even appeared in front of the British Columbia Human Rights Tribunal in 2008 to answer for an article written for *Maclean's* magazine in 2006, 'The future belongs to Islam', in which Steyn claims that the demographic growth of Islamic populations poses an existential threat to the West (but, you'll be relieved to know, we don't need to worry about Africa because it's 'riddled with AIDs' and its 'primary identity is tribal'). But even foreknowledge of the *Post*'s longstanding animosity towards HRCs couldn't fully stymy the sense of surprise at the extent of their full-court press for Peterson. Christie Blatchford praised Peterson, breathlessly, as a 'warrior for common sense and plain speech' and 'a hurricane of fresh air'. Rex Murphy made his best attempt to surmise who might be the true victim in the situation—Peterson is, of course—before calling him 'an actual, a real, university professor' (which is definitely, definitely true). And Conrad Black, the *National Post*'s thoughtful albeit prolix founder[6] and a man who served 42 months in prison[7] for defrauding the investors in its parent company, tried his hand at gender studies: 'All people must be treated with respect, equally. But there are only two genders, two sexes; our species and all other mammals are "gender-binary".' Of the *National Post*'s regular contributors to pass word on Peterson in this period, only Chris Selley abstained from issuing a glowing appraisal, instead noting wryly that academic freedom should provide for Peterson's right to be 'a total jerk'.

Due to the scandal at the University of Toronto and the accompanying right-wing media oversell, Peterson managed to, in October 2016 alone, roughly double the number of views his videos received on YouTube, racking up 1.5 million in this period. And—surprise, surprise—many of those who identified with Peterson's message hailed from the 'alt-right', a burgeoning reactionary subculture that evolved out of the septic annals of Reddit subforums and white national Word Presses (and that, in October 2016, was in the throes of playing an important role in helping deliver the presidency to Donald Trump). Certainly, if Peterson had any qualms about being fêted by this audience, he was far from adamant in expressing them. When asked to give his opinion about the 'ethnic nationalism' advocated by the alt-right during an appearance in March 2017 at the Ottawa Public Library[8], he managed to muster just a few mild criticisms, characterizing their philosophy as 'incomplete' in so far as it's based on a 'benevolent' desire to 'reconstitute the father' that goes too far in its valorization of an authoritarian statist ethos and thereby fails to 'become the son' (he also notes with disapproval the alt-right's 'continual proclivity to degenerate into anti-Semitism', including 'in the comments, for example, on my videos'). But this came after months of tweets and public statements that seemed practically tailored to play to that audience. On 17 December 2016, on Twitter, for instance: 'Women: if you usurp men they will rebel and fail and you will have to jail or enslave them.'[9] And besides, if the alt-right is just sorely in need of a parent capable of instilling in them an anti-statist zeal, what does that make Peterson?

Peterson's appeal to the alt-right, however, had more to do

with just the content of his ideas. For it also has to do with the *way* in which he expresses them. Much of the alt-right is comprised of, as should be obvious to everyone by now, white men who are frustrated by the status quo—a status quo that's based on a continued diminution of the middle class coupled with the steady advancement in the economic and social achievement of previously marginalized populations: women, persons of colour, etc (that white, male industrial workers were disproportionately affected by the job losses that occurred in the wake of the 2007-08 recession cannot be understated in its importance, should one wish to trace the genealogy of the alt-right). It's easy enough, then, to apply a glib Marxist analysis and note that many of the alt-right's adherents seek to falsely establish a causal relationship between the two abovementioned terms, in effect *blaming* minorities for the spavined state of Western society. But what's more interesting is how Peterson, specifically, fits into this equation. For if Trump's appeal derives partly from the fact he's a winner and a loser at the same time—that his grotesque life, magnified by his grotesque wealth, can only manifest as an offence to liberal aesthetes, thereby perversely allowing him to pass himself off as a spokesperson for the downtrodden—the same can be said, up to a point, of Peterson. Peterson, of course, isn't as vulgar as Trump: he *was* an Ivy League professor. But when he speaks, he nevertheless speaks with the stern, condemnatory tone of a man who feels—who knows, even—that his ideas will never garner the unqualified approval of the intellectual establishment. 'There was plenty of motivation to take me out,' Peterson would later remark to *British GQ* in 2018. 'It just didn't work.' Like America's beleaguered president, whose only means of voiding controversy is by engendering more of it, Peterson's celebrity has been built upon an edifice of emotional outbursts directed against him. And for someone to be so opposed by so many, they must be saying something important. Right?

To say that Peterson's thought has never garnered the

'unqualified approval' of the intellectual establishment doesn't mean that it wasn't complicit in its propagation. For while a self-appointed crusader against bureaucratically-imposed political correctness, the irony is that Peterson was *created* by that same bureaucracy (this is a significant part of what gives him his soupcon of authority—compare Peterson with, e.g. Steven Crowder; an alt-right luminary who built his career engaging in recorded debates on political topics with often stoned-seeming first-year college students). This is true of his academic heritage, which saw his ideas pass muster at publicly-funded institutions from Harvard to the University of Toronto. It's also true of his transition into being an omnipresent voice on the Canadian media circuit, which was facilitated through appearances on publicly-funded networks such as tvo and CBC. Nor is his indebtedness to Canadian-statist ideology even particularly subtle: his obsession with the theme of genocide, for instance— by the end of Chapter Five of *Maps of Meaning*, after Solzhenitsyn, Frankl, et al., one just about expects him to start quoting from *The Diary of Anne Frank*—is total kitsch Canadiana. Yet while Canadian public school students are assigned a steady stream of texts about ethnic massacres and dystopic collective projects— from *1984* to *Lord of the Flies*—in order to disabuse them of the notion that opposing the nation's faux-benevolent liberal order could ever yield positive results, Peterson effectively *inverts* this logic, arguing that the politically-correct state has become the same authoritarian monstrosity it inveighs against. Given the social tensions that permeate Canadian society—in particular, the disdain felt by many towards the country's morally sanctimonious ruling neoliberal idiocracy—that such a move would curry favour that is unsurprising. But the predictability of Peterson won't make his influence any easier to quell, in Canada or elsewhere: it being much easier to *prevent* the development of these ideas in the first place than to *stop* them once they've already become thoroughly entrenched. When you've taught people to sound the tocsin of totalitarianism at the slightest warning for years, what do you do when it's sounded on you?

Conclusion: Political Correctness, Prejudiced Directness

Well, for starters, you acknowledge how you got there in the place. Rhetorically, Peterson is at his strongest, his most world-beating, when he points out the contradictions that undergird our existing liberal dispensation: the way that, to give an example at random, Canadian state multicultural policy ignores the blatant necessity of instilling a society with a common set of values (albeit with some permitted variances), lest it degenerate into civil infighting. Of course, in practice, it *is* the case that Canada, like any nation, has an overarching set of common values—a fact that often goes unacknowledged by politicians. But the very fact that this dream of a rhizomatic society was ever disingenuously promised tells us a great deal about how liberal ideology functions: the way that its promise of transcendence, its privileging of rights over obligations, must always run afoul of social reality. The solution to this conundrum is not, as Peterson would have it, banally asserting the need for a rehabilitation of 'Western' values. Nor is it affirming the desirability of incorporating the practices of all different cultures into a national framework—a ludicrous notion, to be sure. Rather, it lies in committing ourselves to the creation of a cultural landscape that is neither/nor—neither 'traditionally Western' in the sense meant by Peterson (though certainly 'Western' in a more radical, emancipatory sense), nor a mere composite of heterogeneous cultures endowed with their own respective chauvinisms.

Peterson's arguments, then, are impossible to fully refute without also refuting the liberal fallacies they're premised upon. And this is why pointing out the scholarly errors in a text like *12 Rules for Life*—many of which seem to have been added *intentionally* at the last minute in order to court an alt-right audience who, for all their whingeing about elites, are starved for highbrow intellectual validation—will only take us so far. What's required, instead, is to portray the full spectrum upon which Peterson's ideology operates.

Chapter Seven

Exoteric and Esoteric, OR The Terrible Intensity of Peterson

As a Swiss I am an inveterate democrat, yet I recognize that Nature is aristocratic and, what is even more, esoteric.
Carl Jung

Janus-Faced Fascisms

Depending upon whom you ask — or read — you'll normally find that Peterson is presented in one of two ways. On one side, as an unrepentant chauvinist (if not fascist), whose evolutionarily tinged self-help philosophy reprises the worst prejudices of Carl Jung's pseudoscientific mysticism. On the other side, as a benign liberal-conservative, whose calls for men and women alike to toughen up, and for a revaluation of ideas that don't mesh well with the politically-correct consensus, he represents a welcome corrective to decades of overstretching by meddlesome progressives.

As it turns out, neither of these positions does full justice to Peterson. There are, so it goes, plenty of vituperative chauvinists to go around, especially in 2019 — were this all he had to offer, there's simply no way he would've become a fraction as popular as he has (with 3 million copies sold, it's safe to say that not everyone who bought *12 Rules for Life* regularly marches around with tiki torches throwing Seig Heils). On the other hand, portraying Peterson as a thinker devoid of any kind of higher-order ideological agenda, as one who evinces common-sense moderation, is similarly disingenuous. Were Peterson's sole *modus operandi* simply to tell disaffected men to make their beds — something most women would surely be happy about! — he would never have become a crucible for activists at the

University of Toronto, never have been valorized by the right-wing media, never have attracted the rabble of the alt-right.

The truth is that Peterson's appeal stems from his ability to be *both* these things—at once the prosaic, classically liberal public educator reminding us of our duties to others (and ourselves), as well as the hardened reactionary whose books and lectures promise the promulgation of darker truths. This opposition was readily visible at an appearance at Lafayette College on 29 March 2018. When posed a question about whether discrepancies in IQ between different races should be acknowledged[10], Peterson—noting that he's cautious with this issue, as 'you can't do anything about it' without 'immediately being killed'—launches into a long exposition about the way that, as a society, we frequently succumb to 'the tail problem', in which we fail to adequately acknowledge the way that seemingly minor differences between groups can be more thoroughly manifest at extremes (while men are more aggressive than women 60 per cent of the time, the 1 per cent of most aggressive individuals will invariably be male). Yet this was just scaffolding for Peterson's main point: that the fact the average IQ of Ashkenazi Jews is 'somewhere between 110 and 115, which is about one standard deviation above the population average'—a palpable difference, but not one that has a great effect 'in the middle of the distribution'—means that a hugely disproportionate number of 'geniuses' will derive from this population (lauding the superior biological intelligence of Jews being, one imagines, the most politically-correct way to stump for racial science). This is a characteristically clever act of misdirection. For by responding to a question about discrepancies in racial intelligence by opining on a decidedly dryer topic—that of the public misapprehension of statistics—Peterson is able to blunt the impact of the point of view he implicitly puts across: that, yes, races have differing levels of competence and that, yes, this is something that policymakers, and the public at large, should be cognizant of. And even then, he couches this in a disclaimer, concluding by noting that 'there doesn't seem to be any relationship whatsoever between intelligence and virtue' and that one shouldn't take the former as a benchmark of the 'intrinsic value of human beings'.

Peterson's Illiberal Liberalism

There are, of course, plenty of gaps in Peterson's argumentation here. Questions concerning the degree to which IQ can be taken as genuinely indicative of racial heredity, as opposed to socialization, for instance—Peterson even admits that race is notoriously hard to pin down as a biological category—are largely swept under the rug, on the flimsy pretext that IQ testing is 'the best thing we have'. As mentioned before, this is Peterson's fallacy of choice: essentially, the hasty generalization of statistics that gauge observable behaviours as reflective of inborn traits[11]. What's more interesting than surveying Peterson's logical follies, though, is to glean from his Lafayette lecture a sense of the fault line that runs through all of his ideas. *Yes*, Peterson affirms, different levels of racial intelligence are apparent— and, it would seem, passed on biologically. But then there's that disavowal; one that's always tacked on as a postscript to his most tendentious statements: but *no*, you shouldn't actually *predicate society upon it.*

Understanding this disarticulation can go a long way towards helping us gauge exactly what Jordan Peterson means when he self-identifies as a 'classical liberal'. During his response to the question on IQ and race at Lafayette, the good doctor takes both liberals and conservatives alike to task for their shared conviction that there's a 'job for everyone': one that can be obtained either through, as liberals advocate, retraining, or, as conservatives advocate, by said individuals getting 'off their asses' and working (Peterson is presumably not aware of the way his own status as a tenured university professor makes a strong argument for this supposition). By contrast, Peterson assures us, trying his hand as Platonic philosopher-king, there are some people who are too inept and/or antisocial to do much at all—a claim he backs up by citing the way that the US Armed Forces refuses to induct applicants with IQs under 83 on the grounds that they can only be counterproductive, as well as the 'dismal' record of psychologists to correct the behaviour of 'early onset aggressive' kids.

It's hard to fix a definition of liberalism—the term is intrinsically amorphous, making it a convenient watchword for Peterson to file his eclectic worldview under. But if we accept the characterization of liberalism by political philosopher John Gray as being based on the values of individualism, meliorism, universalism and egalitarianism, it's worth noting that, for Peterson, the latter is, at best, a convenient fiction that can be occasionally wielded for useful political purposes. Indeed, nowhere in Peterson do we find the optimism of Adam Smith, who consistently sought to vindicate the judgements of ordinary people, and rationalized capitalist accumulation on the grounds that most anyone, in principle, was endowed with the productive capacity to accrue wealth. Nor do we even find anything akin to the admission, made by Hobbes in *Leviathan*, that even if some are stronger and wiser than others at least virtually everybody has the ability to *kill somebody else* (as Peterson's point about the Armed Forces suggests, many it would seem—the 10 per cent of the population with IQs under 83, to be precise—are even *too dumb* for that). Instead, what we find in Peterson is a valorization of liberal capitalism as the best system at our disposal on the grounds that, while it produces inequality, it does so in a manner Peterson imagines as broadly consistent with nature. We quote here from *12 Rules for Life*'s oft-parodied first chapter (or—since Peterson seems to actually expect us to take this stuff seriously— 'rule') on lobsters, 'Stand up straight with your shoulders back':

When a defeated lobster regains its courage and dares to fight again it is more likely to lose again than you would predict, statistically, from a tally of its previous fights. Its victorious opponent, on the other hand, is more likely to win. It's winner-take-all in the lobster world, just as it is in human societies, where the top 1 per cent have as much loot as the bottom 50 per cent—and where the richest eighty-five people have as much as the bottom three and a half billion.

This principle is sometimes known as Price's law, after Derek J. de Solla Price, the researcher who discovered its application in science in 1963. It can be modelled using an approximately L-shaped graph, with number of people on the vertical axis, and productivity or resources on the horizontal.

This standpoint goes hand-in-hand with Peterson's view of nature as pitiless in general:

> It is also a mistake to conceptualize nature romantically. Rich, modern city-dwellers, surrounded by hot, baking concrete, imagine the environment as something pristine and angelic, like a French impressionist landscape. Eco-activists, even more idealistic in their viewpoint, envision nature as harmoniously balanced and perfect, absent the disruptions and depredations of mankind. Unfortunately, 'the environment' is also elephantiasis and guinea worms (don't ask), anopheles mosquitoes and malaria, starvation-level droughts, AIDS and the Black Plague.

One can see here that Peterson, while even less convinced of the equitable distribution of competences than Hobbes, clearly shares his view that life outside the confines of society would necessarily be 'solitary, poor, nasty, brutish, and short'. Understandable, then, that—in the above citation—he dismisses what he describes as the romantic conceptualization of nature (a conception apparently harboured by 'Rich, modern city-dwellers' and, especially, 'eco-activists'). Later on in the text—in the fifth 'rule', 'Do Not Let Your Children Do Anything That Makes You Dislike Them', (something Peterson should maybe heed when addressing his ideological progeny on the alt-right)—Peterson elaborates on the philosophical heritage of this conceptualization, offering a cursory critique of Jean-Jacques Rousseau's theorization of the state of nature (and even indulges in ad hominem—a safe move, since Rousseau isn't here to trade rejoinders with him over Twitter):

> The belief that children have an intrinsically unsullied spirit, damaged only by culture and society, is derived in no small part from the eighteenth-century Genevan French philosopher Jean-Jacques Rousseau. Rousseau was a fervent believer in the corrupting influence of human society and private ownership alike. He claimed that nothing was so gentle and wonderful as man in his pre-civilized state. At precisely the same time, noting his inability as a father, he abandoned five of his children to the tender and fatal mercies of the orphanages of the time.
>
> The noble savage Rousseau described, however, was an ideal—an abstraction, archetypal and religious—and not the flesh-and-blood reality he supposed. The mythologically perfect Divine Child permanently inhabits our imagination. He's the potential of youth, the newborn hero, the wronged innocent, and the long-lost son of the rightful king. He's the intimations of immortality that accompany our earliest experiences.

Peterson's critique of Rousseau is somewhat more rigorous than his critique of Bachofen. As proof of nature's barbarity, he cites William Golding (*Lord of the Flies* is a great book!), Jane Goodall's account of the violent inter-tribal warfare of chimpanzees, and the high recorded homicide rates of known hunter-gatherer societies. Of course, there's plenty of anecdotal evidence that could also be used to *support* Rousseau's idyllic account of pre-civilizational society—including Margaret Mead's observation of the relative lack of developmental difficulties experienced by adolescents in Samoan tribal society in *Coming of Age in Samoa* (a text that, in spite of the best efforts of Derek Freeman, has never been successfully debunked). And besides, it's a bit petty to weaponize Goodall's findings against Rousseau when he was *literally the first person* to suggest that humans developed from apes (the term 'noble savage' also never appears in Rousseau's oeuvre—it was, rather, invented by his detractors). But the point here is not to accost Peterson for the limitations of his argumentation, particularly in what amounts to a glorified self-help book. Instead, it's to illustrate that Peterson's dismissal of Rousseau, like his dismissal of Bachofen, serves a clear ideological function. Bachofen must be dispensed with because, if his work contains even a grain of truth, Peterson's effort to essentialize patriarchal myths collapses into a mess of contradictions. And Rousseau must be dispensed with because if the state of nature isn't fundamentally inegalitarian, liberal capitalism ceases to be justifiable on account of its indirect, *representative* function.

The words 'indirect' and 'representative' are used here deliberately. For if liberal capitalism were *identical* in its brutality with the broadly Hobbesian state of nature propounded by Peterson, there wouldn't be much of a reason to support it. Instead, for Peterson, it performs a kind of representative function; one that improves upon our primitive conditions while simultaneously reflecting them: I mean, sure, capitalism is unequal, but so are lobsters, and Steven Pinker has already proven that things are getting better in the main, ha ha right? Absent this representative function, political society risks going sideways into—you guessed it—totalitarianism: embodying, in short, the desire for 'everything unpredictable to vanish' he attributes to the authoritarian personality in *Maps of Meaning*.

This frustration with the supposed inability of progressives to reconcile themselves to facts and logic is never far from the surface with Peterson. In his conclusion to the response to the question on racial IQs posed to him at Lafayette College, he suggests that it is 'highly probable' that 'nature and the fates' do not align with our 'egalitarian presuppositions'. But again, this doesn't mean that 'we' should take intelligence (or IQ) as being representative of the 'intrinsic value' of persons. The royal 'we' employed here is, presumably, intended to refer to civil society—the pressure cooker of liberal capitalism being sufficient, Peterson imagines, to sort people by competences (no less so where competences overlap with race, as with his point about the high number of Jewish people in powerful positions). Even if we naively accept, though, this tidy distinction between competence and institutional bias—as if in a world where the average person of European descent has far more access to educational opportunities than the average person of African descent the two could ever be fully separated—and therefore take as a given the moral permissibility of liberal capitalist 'meritocracy', Peterson still adds a caveat. For the intervention of civil society, he suggests, is warranted as long as it is *benevolent*, as opposed to authoritarian: something implicit in his claim that 'we' have to find a 'worthwhile place in society' for people 'on the lower end of the general cognitive distribution'. The average IQ of Black Americans, it's worth mentioning (though for obvious reasons Peterson does not), is one standard deviation lower than White Americans. Thus, following Peterson, it seems to reason that—in an American context—the individuals on the lower end of the general cognitive distribution that 'we' must find a 'worthwhile place' for will be, disproportionately, black.

The problems with this kind of argument are manifold. Peterson may not be, as his most virulent contractors contend, pushing for the erection of internment camps to house ostensibly less competent races. His above argument does, however, betray a gleeful lack of awareness (in so far as he is ever gleeful) of the way that, in a kind of vicious cycle, the historical assumption of lesser competence has often played a crucial role in prohibiting members of marginalized groups from being exposed to professional and/or social contexts that are eligible to nurture the equalization of partly socio-culturally reflective statistics such as IQ. Amiss in Peterson's thought, then, is the notion that society sometimes must behave in accordance with certain regulative ideas—not because they *reflect* the existing state of things, but because it can be reasonably assumed that adherence to them will help lead to the achievement of a level of equality that is currently foreclosed by a multiplicity of cultural and institutional barriers. Such a move is, again, foreclosed by Peterson's ideology. For to attempt too overtly to bring society in line with our 'egalitarian presuppositions', risks leading us down the pathway of totalitarianism. We have, therefore, only limited justifiable means at our disposal to cushion the inegalitarian structure of nature with…

The Psychoanalytic Structure of Disavowal

We can say that there are, then, in effect, two Petersons. There is the exoteric Peterson, who defends the preservation of a liberal capitalist order which allots a limited measure of dignity to all peoples. Then there is the esoteric Peterson, who knows that— regardless of whatever efforts are made—nothing remotely close to real equality, economic or otherwise, will *ever* be successfully cultivated, due to the fact that the tendency to create unequal dispensations is hardwired into nature itself. This opposition, which at first seems contradictory, is in fact intrinsic to the psychoanalytic structure of his work. 'Order', understood as the zeal for rationalization, must be counterpoised with 'chaos' in order for social systems to function harmoniously. These two terms, 'order' and 'chaos', are synonymous with the roles of the 'conscious' and 'unconscious' respectively in the works of Carl

Jung. Take Jung's effort to engage in a re-evaluation of the role of the unconscious in the first chapter of his 1933 *Modern Man in Search of a Soul* (a text Peterson has singled out as having been particularly important to his development):

> It is well known that the Freudian school presents the unconscious in a thoroughly depreciatory light, just as also it looks on primitive man as little better than a wild beast. Its nursery-tales about the terrible old man of the tribe and its teachings about the 'infantile-perverse-criminal' unconscious have led people to make a dangerous monster out of the unconscious, that really very natural thing. As if all that is good, reasonable, beautiful and worth living for had taken up its abode in consciousness! Have the horrors of the World War really not opened our eyes? Are we still unable to see that man's conscious mind is even more devilish and perverse than the unconscious?

Whereas for Freud, the unconscious is comprised of ideas that have been forced out of consciousness by a process of repression, for Jung the unconsciousness is populated by memories derived from our individual and ancestral pasts. This division—between the individual and the ancestral—is accounted for by Jung's separation of the unconscious into two subcategories: that of the personal unconscious and the collective unconscious. Though to describe the inherited traits (or archetypes) that Jung attributes to the collective unconsciousness as 'memories' is already to take a position in a vigorous scholarly debate. Peterson, for instance, in the fifth chapter of *Maps of Meaning*, adopts the position that the collective unconsciousness does not consist of *memories*. Instead, he argues somewhat vaguely, it is composed of 'complexes', which [Jung] defined as heritable propensities for behaviour or for classification—though Peterson admits that 'his writings, which are very difficult, do not always make this clear'. This position is reiterated a few pages later, when Peterson characterizes Jung as 'having believed that many complexes had an archetypal (or universal) basis, rooted in biology, and that this rooting had something specifically to do with memory' — an indication that he finds complexes provide a more suitable basis upon which to ground his neurobiological take on Jung than archetypes per se.

In the above citation from *Modern Man in Search of a Soul*, one can see that Jung — in his own view, at least — has a more favourable view of the unconscious than Freud. This is connected with what Jung views as Freud's underestimation of the importance of religion. For Freud, religion is a 'collective neurosis', one that serves no present-day role in the advancement of society. For Jung, by contrast, religion is not just productive to the everyday lives of believers — it is also a natural expression of the unconscious; one inextricable from the tendency of humans to be endowed with the 'archetype' of God. Untempered by such symbols, consciousness — or rationality — can easily manifest as unfettered destruction, with Jung giving 'the horrors of the World War' as an example. In the ninth chapter of *Modern Man in Search of a Soul* — 'Basic Postulates of Analytical Psychology' — Jung remarks on the historical context that fostered the neglect of spirituality by the discipline of psychology:

Under the influence of scientific materialism, everything that could not be seen with the eyes or touched with the hands was held in doubt; such things were even laughed at because of their supposed affinity with metaphysics. Nothing was considered 'scientific' or admitted to be true unless it could be perceived by the senses or traced back to physical causes. This radical change of view did not begin with philosophical materialism, for the way was being prepared long before. When the spiritual catastrophe of the Reformation put an end to the Gothic Age with its impetuous yearning for the heights, its geographical confinement, and its restricted view of the world, the vertical outlook of the European mind was forthwith intersected by the horizontal outlook of modern times. Consciousness ceased to grow upward, and grew instead in breadth of view, as well as in knowledge of the terrestrial globe.

Peterson shares with Jung this appraisal of the spiritual emptiness of 'modern man' (not to mention the limitations of materialist thought). But, as you might expect from someone who thinks Jung's theory of the collective unconsciousness can be *proven* with the aid of neuroscience, he is more circumspect in his endorsement of religion. Instead what he offers us, with *12 Rules for Life* in particular, is a thinly veiled secularization of it; one that promises an 'Antidote to Chaos' in its subtitle, and could sit unobtrusively beside other self-help manuals at an airport off-licence. That the popularity of Peterson's work, accordingly, owes to a range of conundrums particular to our era—pervasive economic precarity, especially among youth; the incapacity to fill the void left by the spectacular collapse of organized religion; the scourge of modern feminism—is so obvious, and has been so widely remarked in shallow online think pieces, that it barely warrants repeating here.

The All-Devouring Archetype

All of this raises the question, however: given Peterson's obsession with the perceived excesses of feminism, how can it be that, when he expresses his political views, they so often centre upon the *need* for chaos, which he characterizes (after Jung) as archetypally feminine? First of all, it's necessary to point out here that 'chaos', according to Peterson, is not *literally* feminine, but rather *symbolically* feminine (though given that he's claimed that 'the SJW sort of "equality above all else" philosophy is more prevalent among women', it's not clear how seriously we can take this). This is due to the fact that femininity is archetypally associable with the 'birthplace of things' — that is, nature. Nature, for Peterson, is intrinsically chaotic. Though it is not just that. For while nature exists under the sign of chaos, it also is endowed with a harmonic aspect — one that Peterson associates, in his political commentaries, with the statistical consistency of differential production (which he explains by way of 'Price's Law'). Like Jung, then, Peterson views nature as both 'aristocratic' and 'esoteric' — aspects that make it ultimately irreconcilable with our 'egalitarian presuppositions'.

This may seem confusing. Putting aside questions about the basic coherency of this worldview, though, we should state that it certainly does align with a core tenant of psychoanalysis; one rooted in German Idealism — that everything belies its opposite[12]. 'Chaos' and 'order', for Peterson, can be best understood as meta-archetypes which are isomorphic to the left and right sides of the brain respectively. They are, further, identifiable with the archetypes of the 'Great Mother' (chaos) and 'Great Father' (order) — with the mediating role of consciousness between the two sides of the brain (*Logos*) represented by the archetype by the 'Divine Son' (undergirding these, additionally, is the 'precosmogonic chaos' of 'pure (latent) information, before it is parsed into the world of the familiar', represented by the archetype of 'uroboros', the 'dragon of chaos'). Nature, as Peterson assures us, does, like the mother, assure certain securities. But it also manifests chaotically — indeed, this is its principle meta-archetypal association. One expression of this chaos can be found in the archetype of the 'devouring mother'. This archetype indexes to the tendency of the site of the originary — nature, or the maternal — to behave in such a suffocating fashion towards its progeny that it *prevents* their individuation; their achievement of synthesis between order (paternal) and chaos (maternal). On a literal, familial level, this is characteristically counteracted, Peterson asserts in the third chapter of *Maps of Meaning*, by the cultivation of group rituals intended to sever the 'dependency [of boys] upon their mothers' that 'often [takes] place under purposefully frightening and violent conditions'.

It probably won't be hard for the astute reader to guess where this is going. But anyway, here goes: the modern politically-correct state, beholden as it is to 'SJW activists', embodies, in Peterson's view, the archetype of the devouring mother. This position is spelled out clearly in an article published in *The Toronto Sun* on 29 March 2018—a paper best known in Canada for splashy covers that often indulge in left-wing scare-mongering, extensive sports coverage and pictures of scantily-clad women ('Sunshine Girls'—a feature inspired by the topless photos of British tabloids, but that due to some stroke of North American moralism, ended up only with pictures of women fully-clothed). In the article, titled, in all caps, 'MOST DANGEROUS WOMAN IN CANADA', Peterson offers his opinion on the then-sitting premier, Kathleen Wynne[13] (the politician he erroneously attributed blame to during the controversy over Bill C-16 for enforcing 'compelled speech'). Like Justin Trudeau—a '"Peter Pan" prime minister'—Wynne, for Peterson, represents a deviation from the archetypal order our society ought to adhere to. Wynne is certainly 'not a Liberal'. Moreover, 'Everyone in Ontario is not her grandchild, We're not infants...We don't need that much compassion and her insistence on identity politics is unacceptable. The things that have happened under her watch at the universities are unacceptable, they're way worse than people think.' And in case it wasn't wholly clear for his followers which archetype he was filing Wynne under, he retweeted the same day of its publication with the attached headline: 'Our devouring mother...'

The 'devouring mother', then, for Peterson—amongst whose ranks include Kathleen Wynne and the obese sea witch in *The Little Mermaid*—appears as the guardian of order. But in fact, her insistence upon infantilization of her offspring can only lead, conversely, to its diminution: to a totalitarianism that blocks the prospect of individuation. In this way, while the 'devouring mother' ostensibly opposes herself to the 'reality of differential production', in practice she aggravates it by preventing the exposure of 'The Divine Son' to the volatile conditions that enable his development. What we have here, then, is chaos— not to be confused with the ur-chaos of the uroboros—disguised as un-chaos: the commitment to an asinine order that can only terminate in disorder.

Lest anyone think we've been overly uncharitable to Peterson, they should be consoled to know that the above explanation represents a thoroughgoing effort to make sense of aspects of his work that are wholly consistent. All of this, of course, helps shed light on the esoteric/exoteric dyad that informs much of Peterson's work—the way the 'chaos' of nature must be *represented* in the structuration of society, so as, paradoxically, to be staved off. This duality also applies to Peterson's views on race—views that come close in certain respects to those of Jung. Whether Jung can be genuinely regarded as a thinker of 'race' remains, to this day, a significant source of debate. By his own admission, 'archetypes are not determined as regards their content, but only as regards their form, and then only to a very limited degree'. As such, they manifest differently depending on the social and political context in question. One should not, then, you would think, mistake the archetype for the image, as this conflation risks leading to the promulgation of pernicious stereotypes. Yet in spite of this warning, Jung often fails to take his own advice, and consistently cites non-white peoples as living embodiments of the primitive state of mind (black Africans in particular). Such a view is connected with the notion, championed by Jung but discredited within modern psychology, of 'recapitulation'—that in the process of individuation, a member of a more advanced species must progress through the previous stages experienced by a less advanced one.

Peterson is not, by any conventional metric, vigorously racist. But the notion of 'recapitulation' does surface rather conspicuously within his work. In the previously cited argument against the idyllic, Rousseauean state of nature for instance, he invokes both the 'terrible intensity of the schoolyard' and the 'much more murderous' character of hunter-gatherer societies in the same breath in order to demonstrate the darkness that, we're meant to believe, dwells within the human soul. His description of the high homicide rate in hunter-gatherer societies is followed immediately by an observation that renders the implicit comparison he's put forth—between children and tribal communities, and Jung's 'archaic man'—explicit:

> Because children, like other human beings, are not only good, they cannot simply be left to their own devices, untouched by society, and bloom into perfection. Even dogs must be socialized if they are to become acceptable members of the pack—and children are much more complex than dogs. This means that they are much more likely to go complexly astray if they are not trained, disciplined and properly encouraged.

The 'terrible intensity' of unsocialized children? What about the terrible intensity of Peterson? Chilling remarks such as these can be—given that Peterson often puts them forth as prosaically as, say, a science teacher explaining to his students why sugar dissolves in water—easily overlooked. Taken cumulatively, however, they suggest a serious underlying contradiction in his work. In *Maps of Meaning*, Peterson—in order to safeguard Jung's theory of the collective unconscious from charges of irrationalism that can be easily levelled at it—attempts to explain, as we've mentioned before, archetypes by way of neurobiology. This is a view that would, you would think, force him to commit to a more *deflationary* view of them than Jung—that is, to live up to

Jung's injunction that they should be treated 'as regards their form' rather than 'as regards their content'. Peterson perhaps *imagines* he is doing this. But worth noting is the astonishing frequency with which his use of archetypes indexes back, in practice, to the same old ragbag of early twentieth-century prejudices (though the post-2007/08 era may wish to modestly object to its exclusion from this competition). For Peterson, this is just a matter of *science*. But unless you really think that the high homicide rates in hunter-gatherer societies make their members commensurable with empathically underdeveloped children, or that women are more likely to subscribe to 'the SJW sort of "equality above all else" philosophy' because of an evolutionary-psychological fixation on 'distribution',[14] it's likely you'll find that Peterson's appeals to the canon of science tell us more about him—and our politically sordid times—than it.

Conclusion: Peterson's Forsworn Shadow

For Jung, 'the shadow' refers to the unconscious—the way that it always trammels up what consciousness cannot, often becoming a repository of our darkest, animal instincts. It's perhaps this way that we can best understand Peterson: as a thinker whose frequent disavowals of the alt-right betray an unsettling similarity; a projection onto others of something his ego cannot identify with. This similarity is not apparent in the exoteric side of Peterson's work—the platitudinous endorsements of milquetoast liberal capitalism that he's so fond of. But they are apparent in his deeply autarchic and biocentric view of the natural world, one that he often seems to dare audiences with.

Sometimes, Peterson spells out this opposition bluntly. In a 21 March 2018 appearance on the podcast *Matt Lewis & the News*—when asked whether he would've voted for Trump or Hillary—Peterson stammers a bit. But then he concedes: 'I think...I would've impulsively voted for Trump at the last moment'—but not, he makes sure to add, 'with a sense of delight'. What follows is several minutes of back-and-forth in which Peterson appears to concur that Trump's use of identity politics—albeit right-wing identity politics—mirrors efforts by the Left to 'retribalize' society, and chides Hillary as being the candidate of 'conniving scripting lies' contra Trump's 'unscripted impulsive lies' (he also, fascinatingly, expresses his disappointment with the Democrats for their abandonment of the working class—something he attributes partly to the fact he comes from a 'somewhat working-class background'). Likewise: 'what bothers me about Peterson', a disaffected fan writes in the Facebook group 'Dr Jordan B. Peterson's Mythopoeic PARTY BOAT'—which, as of 2019, largely functions as an online stockroom of Pepe the Frog memes and articles by alt-right academics like Ricardo Duchesne—'is that's he [sic] always goddamn fence-sitting'. Considering Peterson's own professed disdain for hypocrisy, can we blame his followers for taking his thought to what seems to be its apotheosis? If individuals such as these are Peterson's shadow, this much is clear: he casts a long shadow over them, too.

Chapter Eight

The Spectre of Post-Modern Neo-Marxism

A spectre is haunting our Earth: the spectre of Postmodern Neo-Marxism. All of the forces of the far right have united and entered into a holy alliance to exorcise this spectre: 4chan and 8chan, Trump and Orban, Neo-Nazis and shitposters...

Marx's Steady Haunting

If playing mad libs with the first two sentences of *The Communist Manifesto* could be construed as a clichéd way to start a chapter, this is only a symptom of a larger issue: that it's a cliché to talk about Marx. Indeed, 28 years after the fall of the Soviet Union—dubbed by the global media as the *coup de grâce* to communist hypothesis—Marx continues to incite and allure us; to bedevil us with his spectre. Perhaps the surest proof of this lies in the frequency with which the terms 'Marxist' or 'socialist' continue to be employed as scare words by the Right. Brazil's Bolsonaro has claimed his educational reforms are geared at purging 'Marxist rubbish' from classmates, and that climate change is a conspiracy forged by 'cultural Marxists' to aid China. Trump has spoken in disquieting tones of an alt left that menaces America, and asserted that: 'We will never be a Socialist or Communist Country' (and that 'IF YOU ARE NOT HAPPY HERE, YOU CAN LEAVE!'). We mentioned before Jung's notion of 'the shadow'—of the repressed content of the personal unconscious with which the ego cannot identify. This, clearly, is ours.

There appear to be two major reasons for Marxism's enduring influence. The first of these is that, like Jay-Z during his post-*Black Album* 'retirement', it never really went away in the first place—particularly in its Maoist iteration[15]. China is poised to soon become the largest economy in the world. And

152

while functionally capitalist in many ways, it still relies on an extensive regime of bureaucratic controls and SOEs (state-owned enterprises) to ensure its stability. Maoists in Nepal helped spur the collapse of the monarchy there in 2006. And Indian Naxalite guerrillas continue to be active in 20 of the nation's 28 states, carrying on a rebellion that started in 1967—and that shows no signs of abating.

The second is that, while the hypothesis that Marxism had been consigned to the dustbin of history after '91—a hypothesis crystallized in Fukayama's 1991 *The End of History and the Last Man*—relied on a conflation of Marxism with state communism, Marx's theories in fact have a far broader resonance. Contrary to popular belief, Marx never left a 'blueprint' for how one should go about politically constructing a communist state (in this matter, Lenin, Mao, etc. were on their own). But he did, in *Capital*, adroitly show how the contradictions inherent to capitalism must lead inexorably to its demise. Chief among these was the notion that a gradually falling rate of profit would engender widespread automation—widespread automation that would then lead to a stark disparity between rich and poor, inflaming revolutionary tensions. Few could deny that, in the aftermath of 2007-08, these predictions seem unsettlingly prescient. Indeed, even the lynchpins of the capitalist economy don't seem to be bothering to deny it anymore. Take the Governor of the Bank of England, Mark Carney: 'Marx and Engels may again become relevant...If you substitute platforms for textile mills, machine learning for steam engines, Twitter for the telegraph, you have exactly the same dynamics as existed 150 years ago—when Karl Marx was scribbling the Communist Manifesto.'

The Rhetorical Figure of Communism

Of course, the collapse of the Soviet Union still *did* have the consequence of depressing the fortunes of would-be Marxist revolutionaries worldwide. How could it not have? Its spectacular demolition, the secession of its browbeaten member-states, and the relinquishing of state-economic planning by much of the Third World had effects in even relatively *bourgeois* environs, as once formidable communist parties in France and Italy tumbled headlong into the electoral gutter. It also had an effect on the way its enemies *spoke* about Marxism. Once a term applied indiscriminately to Marxists and non-Marxists endowed with progressive instincts alike, after '91, the vaporization of actual self-avowed communist organizations in the West rendered accusations of 'Marxism' increasingly parodic. Indeed, for the most part *the only ones* visible enough to be tarred with the label had already taken pains to distance themselves from its dogmas. Not that this made a difference, for the frequently deluded minds, and mouthpieces, of the Right. Social democratic parties that had committed themselves to, at most, moderate Keynesian programmes? Potentially Marxist. Ecological activists, perpetuating the hoax of global warming in order to covertly augment the role of the state? Marxists. Academics who seem suspiciously over concerned with questions of race and gender? *Definitely* Marxists. By the time actual Marxism began its slow march back to popular relevance in the West—in the instability that gripped society after 2007-08—the fact that almost exclusively non-Marxists had been so long the recipients of this kind of abuse, coupled with the waxing influence and lunacy of the far right, made it only natural to (yet again) roll both groups together. Thus, in a retconning of a fascist diction, an array of new terms began to surface online, that could be used to lump together both Marxists and anyone interested in advancing the lot of literally anyone who was marginalized (and not, to borrow from intersectional jargon, a cis white male). The most famous, of course, being—in a weird nod to Gramsci—'cultural Marxist'.[16]

It is in this context that Jordan Peterson, transformed from fringe crank academic to cultural behemoth by the scandal surrounding Bill C-16, entered the popular fray. Mentioned before was that it seems likely that Peterson and his editors—during the year-and-a-half or so that fell between the controversy regarding 'compelled speech' that erupted at the University of Toronto and the publication of *12 Rules for Life*—tweaked the book so as to make its contents appeal to the young (or at least perpetually adolescent) reactionary set that had so thoroughly embraced his message. Whether this is true or not, upon its publication, *12 Rules for Life* came endowed with its own historically falsifiable one-size-fits-all narrative that sought to yoke together the pieties of post-modern identity politics and the 'murderous' legacy of Marxism into one, ominous foe. Presumably wanting to avoid directly echoing the verbiage of the alt-right, Peterson, with characteristic carefulness, does not call this hybrid 'cultural Marxism'—though the premise is, give or take a few details, largely the same. Instead, apropos his academic stature, he elects for a wordier term: that of 'postmodern neo-Marxism'.

When in Need, Invent a Neologism

What is, then, 'postmodern neo-Marxism'? The adjective 'postmodern' is crucial here, since, to a greater extent than his (disavowed) fellow travellers on the alt-right, Peterson's account stresses the role that French poststructuralist— post-modern, as they're often broadly described—intellectuals played in reshaping academic cultures in North America and elsewhere (a hilarious consequence of which being that in many ways Peterson's take is even *less* accurate than the screeds published by online ideologues, who tend to lay more emphasis on bona fide Marxists like Gramsci or Horkheimer). Given Peterson's status as a professor who's spent much of his life attempting to rationalize the prejudicial aspects of Jung's thought via an appeal to neurobiology, this stress is wholly unsurprising. Marxists, after all, never had much of a foothold in the North American academic establishment (and certainly not in Canada, a state that would've never afforded a self-identifying Marxist intellectual the same support that was pivotal in Peterson's elevation to popular acclaim). But poststructuralists—among whose ranks are usually cited Jacques Derrida and Michael Foucault, among others—do. The relativistic critiques of these thinkers—whose ideas vary greatly, but who shared in common a rejection of the scientific pretensions of the structuralism dominant in France in the early-mid-1960s—in turn made them, and their followers, the bane of many Anglophone academics, who often charged their ideas with being a threat to the notion of epistemic certitude *tout court* (and, thus, the academy).

Considering the timeline of Peterson's academic career— essentially, from the 90s onward—it's likely that, at least up until the recent revival in interest, *actual* Marxists didn't pose much of a threat to his ability to disseminate his ideas. Even with his threadbare knowledge of the subject, he was astute enough, however, to notice that many of the cultural changes that gripped universities in this time—spurred on by the tremendous demographic diversification of North American student bodies, among other factors—took *some kind of influence* from the poststructuralist canon. One can, though, so it's said, find red on Betsy Ross' flag, should they look hard enough (and this goes for Jacques-Louis David's tricolour, too). And so with great perspicacity Peterson, through an extensive study of what appears to be exclusively secondary literature written by conservative hacks, came to a realization: *the poststructuralists were educated by Marxists*. And, what's more, *they talked about Marxism*, sometimes in a way that wasn't even openly condemnatory. Thus, with a few logically dissociative leaps, we get passages such as these in *12 Rules for Life*:

...Important in recent years has been the work of French philosopher Jacques Derrida, leader of the postmodernists, who came into vogue in the late 1970s. Derrida described his own ideas as a radicalized form of Marxism. Marx attempted to reduce history and society to economics, considering culture the oppression of the poor by the rich. When Marxism was put into practice in the Soviet Union, China, Vietnam, Cambodia and elsewhere, economic resources were brutally redistributed. Private property was eliminated, and rural people forcibly collectivized. The result? Tens of millions of people died.

This did not mean that the fascination Marxist ideas had for intellectuals—particularly French intellectuals—disappeared. It merely transformed. Some refused outright to learn. Sartre denounced Solzhenitsyn as a 'dangerous element.' Derrida, more subtle, substituted the idea of power for the idea of money, and continued on his merry way. Such linguistic sleight-of-hand gave all the barely repentant Marxists still inhabiting the intellectual pinnacles of the West the means to retain their worldview. Society was no longer repression of the poor by the rich. It was oppression of everyone by the powerful.

Peterson's (Non-)Reading of Derrida

How does one start? So much of this is bound to cause agony and intellectual offence, starting with the surreal claim that Derrida is the 'leader of the postmodernists' (who are 'the postmodernists'? Do they cast ballots to choose their 'leader'? Or did they have something less banal in mind?). Derrida was in 'vogue' in the late 1970s—though earlier, too, as the furore generated by his 1966 appearance at Johns Hopkins and his mention in Jean-Luc Godard films such as Le Gai savoir (1970) attest to. And while not untrue, Peterson's use of the 'The result?/ Tens of millions of people died' refrain to characterize political Marxism is reductive by his standards.

This is just the first paragraph. The second is, astonishingly, even less coherent. Marx's object of critique was not 'money' but 'capital'—money having enjoyed a long and rich (no pun intended) history that precedes the establishment of the capital relation. Given Sartre's fidelity to the USSR, he surely had an axe to grind with Solzhenitsyn, though in light of the latter's documented aversion to democracy and flirtations with anti-Semitism, it's hard to deny that Sartre might've had a point. 'Power' is not a concept that plays a significant role in Derrida's oeuvre—though it does in Foucault's, a thinker who sought to parlay the Nietzschean 'will to power' into an analytic of power relations that saw them not as exclusively localized in the state but rather as pervading the social field. It's possible, then, that Peterson has his readings mixed up. But if we wanted to be charitable, we could say that Peterson is, with his comments, simply offering a vulgarization of Derrida's view that the historical distinction between writing and speech, and the weighing of one pole over the other, contributed to the crystallization of a multitude of other distinctions—man over woman, for instance, or white over black (though this is not a consequence of writing *per* se, being also dependent on empirical factors). While the particular assignation of the term 'power' to Derrida remains peculiar, this is the general drift of his subsequent commentary:

> According to Derrida, hierarchical structures emerged only to include (the beneficiaries of that structure) and to exclude (everyone else, who were therefore oppressed). Even that claim wasn't sufficiently radical. Derrida claimed that divisiveness and oppression were built right into language— built into the very categories we use to pragmatically simplify and negotiate the world. There are 'women' only because men gain by excluding them. There are 'males and females' only because members of that more heterogeneous group benefit by excluding the tiny minority of people whose biological sexuality is amorphous. Science only benefits the scientists. Politics only benefits the politicians. In Derrida's

view, hierarchies exist because they gain from oppressing those who are omitted. It is this ill-gotten gain that allows them to flourish.

Derrida famously said (although he denied it, later): 'Il n'y a pas de hors-texte' — often translated as 'there is nothing outside the text.' His supporters say that is a mistranslation, and that the English equivalent should have been 'there is no outside-text.' It remains difficult, either way, to read the statement as saying anything other than 'everything is interpretation', and that is how Derrida's work has generally been interpreted.

Certainly, neither Derrida *nor* Foucault thought that 'Science only benefits the scientists' or that 'Politics only benefits the politicians' — such a simplistic take would've been anathema to the more subtle, multi-layered paradigms they erect in order to understand the practical and metaphysical commitments of society. Elucidating the problems with Peterson's reading of Derrida requires more effort than stating this, however. In his 1967 text *Of Grammatology* — the text usually cited as foundational to his thought — Derrida makes a two-fold argument. His first concerns structuralism; a movement indigenous to the field of linguistics (specifically, the work of Ferdinand de Saussure) that attempts to map the linguistically-modelled 'structural networks' that govern culture, and that are distinct from either ideas or existent reality (and that thus function as a 'third order'). In the 'structural Marxism' of Louis Althusser, for instance — and in particular, in his famed essay *Ideology and Ideological State Apparatuses* — Althusser attempts to rework the traditional Marxist distinction between base (means of production) and superstructure (ideology/culture). To do this, he describes the existence of intermediary institutions — ideological state apparatuses (schools, churches, etc.) and repressive state apparatuses (courts, police, etc.) which ensure the conformance of the superstructure with the base (and that, indeed, even supply the conditions through which individuals are *interpellated*—that is, through which they assume their identities). Althusser's positing of the abovementioned institutions—which he uses to demonstrate the 'material existence' of ideology—suggests the influence of the structuralist notion of a 'third order'; a third order that weaves between ideas and reality by indexing the latter to a set of culturally specific significations.

Althusser, of course, is just one of several celebrated French intellectuals whose prodigious theoretical output is responsible for the popularization of structuralism in France in the 1960s: Claude Levi-Strauss, Jacques Lacan, Roland Barthes, etc. all enjoy similarly illustrious legacies. In the first part of *Of Grammatology*, however, Derrida primarily chooses to focus on Ferdinand de Saussure and Claude Levi-Strauss—understandably so, given the former's status as the founder of linguistic structuralism and the latter's importance to its French reception. Derrida's central critique, in this part of the book, regards the Sausserian-derived relation of speech to writing. Writing, for de Saussure, exists for the sole purpose of *representing* speech. Yet what is amiss here, for Derrida, is an acknowledgement of the degree to which written symbols do not have a merely *descriptive* function, that they also play a central role in constituting our understanding of the world (and, indeed, informing the domain of speech). The implications of this thesis stretch far beyond the domain of linguistics (something made particularly clear when one considers the applications of de Saussure's linguistic ideas to other domains, such as with e.g. Levi-Strauss' anthropology). For what structuralism shares in common with Western metaphysics, argues Derrida, is its 'logocentric' structure; that is, a belief in a domain of originary *presence* that representation derives from; one that's existence must be guaranteed through an appeal to 'an absolute logos'. Relinquishing belief in such a guarantor of meaning, then, forces us not only to come to terms with the limitations of structuralism's effort to ˙circumscribe reality—it also forces us to come to terms with the limitations of representation *tout court*. To describe what eludes this process of representation, Derrida—whose argument in *Of Grammatology* owes a great deal to Heidegger's notion of 'Dasein'—uses the term 'the trace' to describe the way that any sign also contains what it *does not* index to (the way 'man' cannot be understood without the correspondent term 'woman', etc.).

The second, and less celebrated part, *Of Grammatology*, deals with Jean-Jacques Rousseau—a strange choice on the surface of things, but one rendered more comprehensible by both Derrida's hostility towards many of the sacred cows of the *patrimoine français* (a hostility that was duly reciprocated by many of its most vehement academic defenders) as well as Rousseau's commentary on linguistics in the *Essay on the Origin of Languages*. Rousseau's analytic of language—not to mention his work more generally—is, for Derrida, based on a 'logic of supplementarity': that is, a consistent tendency to posit a pure origin that is in turn corrupted by the addition of a 'supplement' (such as language). The *Essay on the Origin of Languages* is thus largely characterized by Rousseau's erection of binaries: the way that articulation supplements accent, need supplements passion, etc. Such a view for Derrida ultimately represents a mere *inversion*, rather than *deconstruction*, of the culturally modernizing sensibility that pits new against old, assigning privilege to the former.

Given Derrida's lifelong focus on the limitations of linguistic signification, it's understandable that his signature concept of *différance*—that is, the way that the meaning of any term is infinitely *deferred* through its indexing to other, equally uncertain terms—is often understood as asserting the inescapability of the paradigm of language. Indeed, the notion that Derrida is responsible for aiding is the instigation of a 'linguistic turn' in the field philosophy (and, in turn, the broader culture); one that led to a devaluation of efforts to identify *actual things*, is something that his otherwise highly diverse critics—from disaffected Marxists to philosophical new materialists to cultural conservatives—generally agree upon. Certainly, this is a view shared by Peterson, who in his commentary on Derrida in *12 Rules for Life* trots out a practically tropic misreading of Derrida's claim that 'Il n'y a pas de hors-texte' ('there is nothing outside the text', or 'there is no outside-text') by claiming that what it means is that 'everything is interpretation'. We should give Peterson (or perhaps his editors) an iota of credit here—he at least does not succumb to the most egregious misreading of this phrase, which tends to mistakenly conflate with the advocacy of New Criticism-style close reading. But this is about *all* the credit we can give him. For while there's clearly truth in the claim that Derrida's work ushered in a cultural embrace of linguistic relativism, it's less clear that this popular image of his thought can, *ipso facto*, be taken as adequately descriptive of the scope of his theoretical ambitions. More adequately translated, 'Il n'y a pas de hors-texte' refers to the idea that we cannot *stabilize* a domain of presence that the text can be taken as indexing to— that the meaning of the reality that is ostensibly *outside* is every bit as shifty and elusive as that which lies within. Such a claim needn't be seen, however, as purely epistemic. Indeed, scattered throughout Derrida's oeuvre, there is considerable evidence that the notion of *différance* can be taken as ontologically descriptive of the structure of reality. Nor is this idea confined strictly to Derrida's later texts. In 1966's 'Structure, Sign, and Play in the Discourse of the Human Sciences', for instance, Derrida forcefully delineates the stakes of the deconstructive project, as well as its applicability to science:

> It would be easy enough to show that the concept of structure and even the word 'structure' itself are as old as the *episteme*—that is to say, as old as Western science and Western philosophy—and that their roots thrust deep into the soil of

ordinary language, into whose deepest recesses the episteme plunges in order to gather them up and to make them part of itself in a metaphorical displacement. Nevertheless, up to the event which I wish to mark out and define, structure—or rather the structurality of structure—although it has always been at work, has always been neutralized or reduced, and this by a process of giving it a centre or of referring it to a point of presence, a fixed origin. The function of this centre was not only to orient, balance, and organize the structure—one cannot, in fact, conceive of an unorganized structure—but above all to make sure that the organizing principle of the structure would limit what we might call the play of the structure. By orienting and organizing the coherence of the system, the centre of a structure permits the play of its elements inside the total form. And even today the notion of a structure lacking any centre represents the unthinkable itself. Nevertheless, the centre also closes off the play which it opens up and makes possible.

For Derrida, here, the 'structurality of structure'—the way that 'Western science' and 'Western philosophy' have traditionally depended upon 'a point of presence' that's used to conceptually organize them—could not be thought prior to the intellectual 'rupture' that revealed that 'everything is discourse' (a rupture he identifies with 'the Nietzschean critique of metaphysics', 'the Freudian critique or [sic] self-presence' and 'the Heideggerian destruction of metaphysics' through to French structuralism). There may be the temptation here to take to Derrida's claim that this 'rupture' demonstrated that 'everything is discourse' as tantamount to an affirmation of Peterson's view that he believed 'everything is interpretation'. Derrida's citation of 'Western science' as a domain that 'closes off the play which it opens up and makes possible' should, however, give us pause. For this reflects a constitutive ambiguity that underlies Derrida's critique of this inceptive rupture in 'Structure, Sign and Play'. Figures like Nietzsche, Heidegger and Freud, for Derrida, both denounced metaphysics while discretely *depending* on them: they, in other words, failed to follow their own projects through to their radical conclusion. It is not at all, clear, though, for Derrida, that this radical conclusion is strictly epistemic in its implications (something Derrida's invocation of 'Western science' should clue us to). For could it not be true, as Derrida implies, that the designation of a structural centre also serves as an impediment to the development of the sciences? And if this is the case, would that not indicate that all the contents subsumable by the sciences of the natural world itself, may be devoid of such a centre?

Différance and DNA

The most obvious problem with such a standpoint, of course, is that it risks re-inscribing *différance* as yet another higher-order 'meta-metaphysical' principle, of the type that Derrida set out to critique in 'Structure, Sign, and Play'. It is for this reason, perhaps, that the seminar by Derrida that most explicitly deals with the relationship of deconstruction to science—1975-76's *La vie la mort* [Life Death], which was delivered at the Ecole Normale Superieure—remained unpublished until 2019. In the seminar[17], Derrida discusses in great detail French Nobel prize-winning biologist Francois Jacob's 1975 text *The Logic of Life*—a text that examines the way that the scientific understanding of biology has changed since the sixteenth century (and that pays particular attention to four signal breakthroughs: the discoveries of the functions of organs, cells, chromosomes and genes, and DNA). With characteristic acuity, Derrida outlines what he believes to be a number of questionable metaphysical premises which guide Jacob's inquiry. Most central among these is the way that Jacob defines, in Derrida's view, 're-production' as the 'operative factor' that regulates the logic of life.

This definition, which Derrida traces back to Hegel's claim that 'the living being is living insofar as it can reproduce itself', has the consequence, in his view, of repressing both death and sexual difference. Death, in the sense that Jacob deploys a metaphor—of the way that bacterial cultures 'do not die' but rather 'disappear as individuals: where there was only one, suddenly there are two'—to justify his frequently contradictory view of death as wholly inessential to the primary ontological constituent of life. And sexual difference in the sense that the association made by Jacob between life and reproduction forces him to characterize bacterial reproduction as 'asexual', and thus supplementary, on the grounds that it tends to occur by fission rather than through 'the exchange of genetic material'. Derrida expresses scepticism, as regards the second claim, about the degree to which these exchanges can truly be classified as ancillary, as Jacob insists. And in the case, it is the crazed relativist philosopher, rather than the sober scientist, who has been vindicated by science: in 2006, a paper by Hema Prasad Narra and Howard Ochman, 'Of what Use is Sex to Bacteria?,' demonstrated how the availability of complete bacterial genome sequences furnishes us with proof that exchanges of genetic material between bacteria are more common than previously imagined. But this is not all. The limited capacity for 1:1 reproduction of cells prior to the emergence of living forms, as Jacob explains, is solely ascribable to the regulative function of deoxyribonucleic acid (DNA), which presides over the reproduction of the cell (chemical species, in other words, do not form copies of themselves). Yet, for Derrida, the fact that this internal differentiation is the basis of cellar reproduction shows that there is *already* a reproduction of two terms—and thus, a kind of sexual difference—existent at the level of bacterial fission!

The necessity of this hybridization attests to the way that Derrida's thought cannot be tidily reduced to a declaration of the intertextual structure of reality. For what we see here is a stronger suggestion: that *différance* is in fact a condition of cellular reproduction—and, thus, life in its most embryonic form. And beyond attesting to the possibility of an 'ontological' reading of his oeuvre, Derrida's effort to illustrate the distribution of sexual difference throughout nature, his claim that it cannot be reduced to the supposed ability to 'sexually' reproduce a copy of oneself, has consequences for our current political debate. To recognize the untenability of Jacob's definition, so it goes, is also to recognize that (1) sexual difference is not an ontological determination of humans (nor, more generally, living forms), and 2) that forms of artificial reproduction targeted at liberating sexuality from the somatic domain (in vitro fertilization, ectogenesis, etc.) cannot be occluded on the grounds that they do not meet said criteria. That Derrida not only challenges a scientist—Jacob—on his own terrain, but also, in several respects, gets the better of him, points to an interesting irony. Derrida's ideas, according to Peterson, are defined by a fierce antipathy towards science. 'For Derrida and his post-modern Marxist acolytes,' he declares with hallmark imprecision in 12 Rules for Life, 'science is just another game of power'. Yet in spite of these declarations, and Peterson's associated claim that 'scientific literature' proves 'sex differences are powerfully influenced by biological factors', he has not, to date, succeeded in engaging the question of the scientificity of sexual difference, of consolidating it with his 'system' (a word as inadequate to Derrida as to Peterson, albeit for different reasons) as rigorously as Derrida. Given the ease with which Peterson slips into this kind of polemical posturing, as well as the significance of the question of sexual difference to Jungian psychoanalysis, this probably should—but surely will not—bother him.

Not that it's the only thing that should. Peterson claims, as cited above, that Derrida, in an effort to rebrand Marxism in much the same way that the Coca-Cola Company rechristened Diet Coke as Coke Zero (to sell it to men, hilariously), 'substituted the idea of power for the idea of money, and continued on his merry way'. And what is the smoking gun that Peterson has uncovered that proves the filiation of Derrida's ideas from those of Marx? That while Marx posits that society is defined by the 'repression of the poor by the rich', Derrida, Peterson imagines, merely rejigs this formula a bit, positing 'the oppression of everyone by the powerful'.

The thrust of Derridean deconstruction, as we've already shown, has little to do with the inequitable distribution of 'power' throughout society. But even if it did, it would still be astonishing that someone who cites as liberally from Biblical scripture as Peterson could think that sympathizing with the plight of the dispossessed, or observing the pervasiveness of injustice in the world, is a sufficient criterion for being an adherent of Marx (did God himself merely repurpose the themes of *Capital*, then?). Setting aside these incongruities, though, it is worth noting that Peterson's grossly ideological conflation of deconstruction with Marxism contains, like all untruths, a smidgen of veracity. In his April 2019 debate with the Slovenian Marxist philosopher Slavoj Žižek—a thinker whose frequent digressions into scatology and obscene jokes either burnish or distract from his philosophical bona fides, depending on how elitist you are—Peterson claimed, during a laboured attempt to provide concrete examples of 'postmodern neo-Marxists' (because they don't exist), that: 'I see the connection between the postmodernist types and the Marxists as a sleight-of-hand that replaced the notion of oppression of the proletariat by the bourgeois by the oppression by one identity group by another.' Žižek's response—timed as to deflate Peterson's exposition—drew frantic applause from the unruly segment of non-postmodern neo-Marxists that had assembled to see him in Toronto that night (several of whom had to be ejected over the course of the evening): 'Totally agree with you.'

Derrida Contra the Althusserian Apparatus

Peterson, then, was onto *something*. Identity politics, of course, is not *the same thing* as poststructuralism—even if the former's denial of the possibility of experience outside a hermeneutic frame is partly derived from the latter. But we can, nevertheless, recite Peterson's claims here regarding the relationship of 'postmodernism'—by which he appears to mean French poststructuralism, and Derrida in particular—to Marxism, to see how they stack up.

Certainly, it is true, as Peterson suggests, that the revelation of the atrocities committed under Stalin played a crucial role in alienating several members of the young generation of French intellectuals who later go on to be dubbed 'poststructuralist' from the Parti communiste français (though this alienation was also contributed to by many factors particular to the PCF—the position taken by it on the Algerian War, its condemnation of revolutionary student movements during the events of May 1968, etc). Derrida, for instance, describes his disenchantment with the PCF during a remarkable April 1989 interview with Michael Sprinker that took place at the University of California at Irvine[18]:

> Personally, I saw the Party as being closed up in suicidal politics already then. It was losing. It had two alternatives: either it hardened its Stalinism and would lose through losing its electorate (and therefore become isolated in Europe) or else it would transform into reformism, a moderate socialism of the social democratic type and would lose also, since the Socialist Party already occupied that space. That was the dilemma, the fatal aporia. In a certain sense, [Althusserianism] represented a tough current in the French Communist Party. And from this standpoint, it was even more suicidal than the Party. Although in another sense it was less so because it sought to regenerate a true theoretical thinking to which I

sincerely believe it is correct to pay homage.

As it turned out—and as Derrida later points out in the interview—the PCF would ultimately succumb to the second outcome described in the above response, considerately moderating its positions before experiencing electoral collapse after entering coalition with François Mitterrand's Parti socialiste in 1983-84. Criticisms of the PCF (and their later confirmation) notwithstanding, though, Derrida does profess here qualified admiration for the works of 'structural Marxist' luminary Louis Althusser, whom he describes himself as having interacted with in passing after his enrolment at the Ecole Normale Superieure in 1952 through to when Althusser was forced into mandatory retirement after strangling his wife in a bout of mental illness in 1980 (though in some ways his relationship with Derrida actually becomes *closer* after this, as later Derrida would frequently visit him at the clinic at Epinay-sur-Seine, near Paris). Should we wish to understand the relationship between Derrida and Marxism—or more generally, poststructuralism and Marxism— it will help to dwell on this connection. For even if Derrida by his own admission never took a single course with Althusser, it's very clear, in the interview with Sprinker, that he had developed opinions about Althusserianism during the 1960s:

I had the impression that their concept of history should have passed through the test of this questioning. And I constantly felt not like raising objections but like saying: 'You have to slow down. What is an object? What is a scientific object?' Their discourse seemed to me to give way to a theoreticism or a newfangled scientism that I could have challenged. But, quite naturally, I was paralyzed because at the same time I didn't want my questions to be taken for crude and self-serving criticisms connected with the right or the left—in particular with the Communist Party.

This will require some explanation. For Althusser, Marx, like Galileo or Darwin, effectively discovered a new science; a new 'continent of knowledge'—that of the 'science of history'. Implicit in this science, according to Althusser, was the notion that objects are not, as empiricism proposes, 'just there', awaiting their abstraction. Rather, objects are produced *theoretically*, through the bringing to bear of a conceptual framework upon pre-scientific ideas—a process that results in the 'scientific object' mentioned by Derrida. For Althusser, only 'historical materialism' is endowed with the means to truly furnish us with a scientific comprehension of history. But its achievement of this can be crucially aided by 'dialectical materialism' (Marxist philosophy), which helps to distinguish between ideological concepts and scientific ones. In his most famous texts—*For Marx* and *Reading Capital*, both published in 1965—Althusser attempts to apply this method to Marx himself, engaging in a 'symptomatic' reading of his work that seeks to elucidate the structure of 'Marxist science' (which Althusser claims must be distilled from Marx's writings after his 'epistemological break' of 1845, with *The German Ideology*).

One can see here that Althusser's basic philosophical stance—that Marx was the first one to put history on a scientific footing—is not philosophically demonstrable. To believe it, one must also believe in the veracity of the conceptual framework of Marxism—a framework that views class struggle as the basis of history. Yet this contradiction is, for Althusser, inevitable: all science, he reasons in the appendix of 'Contradiction and Overdetermination', will collapse into an 'epistemological void' should it attempt to produce *'the possibility of its own object and of the concepts corresponding to it'*. For Derrida, however, such philosophically unsatisfying explanations cannot be passed over in silence. Althusser's project may have been relatively sophisticated, in the context of a PCF dominated by Stalinist hacks (and to this extent, Derrida supported it). But it ultimately could not fully answer, in philosophic terms, the questions such as the ones he lays out above: 'What is an object?' 'What is a scientific object?' This is because these questions, Derrida emphasizes in his interview with Sprinker, require recourse to the canon of phenomenology to fully respond to — and in particular, the works of Edmund Husserl and Martin Heidegger. Husserl and Heidegger, of course, were arguably Derrida's two most significant influences: influences without whom Derrida would never have been able to lay out, for instance, his critique of presence in *Of Grammatology*.

These reservations aside, it's possible that Derrida was influenced, to some degree, by Althusser. In the interview, Sprinker, for instance, suggests that the echoes of Althusser's notion of 'symptomatic reading' can be seen in Derrida's textual approach (a suggestion Derrida declines to respond to). What can also be seen in the interview, though, is the way that Derrida believes that Marx's work is irredeemably wed to the history of Western metaphysics:

> Unlike Althusser, I believe that onto-theo-teleology is ineradicable in Marx. Althusser and the Althusserians say, 'Marx is, or must be, Marx, *minus* the onto-theo-teleology, Marx *minus* the eschatology' through an operation that is no longer Marxist, through the *coup de force* of an artificial strategy...But when they do this, there's no point in citing Marx any more or in pretending that Marx *meant-to-say-this* — there's no point, in any case, in lending privilege to that reference and excluding all others. They could perform that gesture without Marx or else with so many others.

As one might expect, Derrida's view — of Marxism as 'onto-theo-teleology' — has implications for his understanding of politics. The shortcomings of Althusser's theoretical project, he suggests, were directly connected to the shortcomings of the communist political one. For while Althusser exerted an admirable effort to try to broaden the scope of Marxist theory, the injunction to adhere to Marx's texts even while subverting them—and by extension, Derrida suggests, Soviet bureaucracy—ultimately obstructed their intellectual force. This does not mean that Marx's work, in Derrida's view, does not warrant analysis (indeed, Derrida decries what he sees as the ongoing marginalization of Marx in French academia). But to do so effectively would require, for Derrida—a Socialist voter, he admits—paradoxically doing so in a manner that is explicitly 'no longer Marxist'.

Ghastly Evaluations

If Derrida's interview with Sprinker occasionally sounds like a book press release, that's because in a certain sense it was. In early 1993, less than 4 years after the interview, Derrida— in the course of just 4 to 5 weeks—dashed off a manuscript for his first (and only) book on Marx, loftily titled *Specters of Marx: The State of the Debt, the Work of Mourning and the New International*. Derrida's timing was, after the book's publication by Galileé later in '93, widely remarked on: why is it that, after vigilantly avoiding the subject of Marxism for the better part of 4 decades, Derrida had chosen to pass comment just over a year after the dissolution of the Soviet Union? As if anticipating this query, Derrida, in *Specters of Marx*, proclaims that the (partial) unshackling of Marxism from its often depraved political context affords a unique opportunity to engage with it anew. If this is hard to argue with, less consensus exists regarding the degree to which, with *Specters of Marx*, Derrida actually *took* this opportunity. For much of *Specters* finds Derrida content to rest on the laurels of his legacy, interpolating passages from *Hamlet* and *The German Ideology* without seriously engaging with Marx's oeuvre, and presenting Marxism as a regulative idea in the vein of his 'democracy to come' (indeed, Bernard Stiegler—one of Derrida's former students, and a renowned philosopher in his own right—would later remark in 2016 that *Specters* 'is not a book about Marx, but a book about Derrida'[19]). At the very least, one could say that this accomplishes a performative function, with Derrida often seeming as indecisive as the vacillating Prince of Denmark himself. But predictably, hard-line Marxists were far from grateful. Accusing deconstruction of being an 'ersatz form of textual politics' that owes its popularity to the fact it 'pulled the rug out from under anything as drearily undeconstructed as solidarity, organization or calculated political action', Terry Eagleton—in the 1999 Sprinker-edited response volume *Ghostly Demarcations*—ruthlessly dismisses *Specters*:

> [Derrida proposes] A 'New International', one 'without status, without title, and without name...without party, without country, without national community...' And, of course, as one gathers elsewhere in the book, without organization, without ontology, without method, without apparatus. It is the ultimate poststructuralist fantasy: an opposition without anything as distastefully systemic or durably 'orthodox' as an opposition, a dissent beyond all formalizable discourse, a promise which would betray itself in the act of fulfilment, a perpetual excited openness to the Messiah who had better not let us down by doing anything as determinate as coming. Spectres of Marxism indeed.

Derrida's response to Eagleton—in the essay 'Marx & Sons', also included in *Ghostly Demarcations*—is wonderfully bitchy. But it's hard to deny here that Eagleton has a point, one made more politely elsewhere in the response volume by authors like Gayatri Spivak and Pierre Macherey. *Specters of Marx* proposes a Marxism strangely emptied of content; one that thereby trespasses the traditional dialectical injunction to achieve equivocity between the rational and the real. Perhaps Derrida, we might generously suggest, was under the sway of his ex-student Catherine Malabou, whose superlative text *The Future of Hegel* argues adroitly for the existence of *voir venir*, or futurity, in that thinker's canon. More cynically, though, it's possible to see the (noble) failure of *Specters* as reflective of the (noble) failure of deconstruction itself—a discipline that radicalized theory at the considerable cost of depriving it of the kind of direct engagement with social reality endorsed by Althusser.

Peterson, Derrida and Big 'B' Being

Ironically, when one considers the idealist aspect of deconstruction—its effort to carry phenomenology to its relativist apotheosis on the terrain of theory—it's quite possible that Derrida and Peterson have more in common than either thinker does with Marx (though *Specters* and a few late career throwaways aside, one cannot equivocate between their respective levels of intellectual rigorousness). Both Derrida and Peterson, unlike Marx, adopt a relativistic view of science—an approach which reflects their intellectual debts to phenomenology and Jung respectively (whereas Marx's more positive appraisal of it derives from Hegel's critique of Romanticism). Likewise, both of them, while not explicitly existential, clearly emerge from a post-Heideggerian (if not post-Schellingian) tradition that emphasizes the contingency of metaphysics, contra—should we accept the common caricature—the more determinant contours of dialectic (though metaphysics is only 'contingent' for Peterson in the sense that its basis is biological as opposed to logical). Heidegger, interestingly, makes exactly one appearance in Peterson's two major texts, in a footnote in *12 Rules for Life* explaining why his use of Being with a capital 'B' is not a mere editorial oversight:

> I use the term Being (with a capital 'B') in part because of my exposure to the ideas of the twentieth-century German philosopher Martin Heidegger. Heidegger tried to distinguish

between reality, as conceived objectively, and the totality of human experience (which is his 'Being'). Being (with a capital 'B') is what each of us experiences, subjectively, personally and individually, as well as what we each experience jointly with others. As such, it includes emotions, drives, dreams, visions and revelations, as well as our private thoughts and perceptions. Being is also, finally, something that is brought into existence by action, so its nature is to an indeterminate degree a consequence of our decisions and choices—something shaped by our hypothetically free will. Construed in this manner, Being is (1) not something easily and directly reducible to the material and objective and (2) something that most definitely requires its own term, as Heidegger labored for decades to indicate.

Never mind the fact that this is, basically, a tabloid of nonsense—whatever else it is, 'Being' for Heidegger is certainly not differentiable from reality 'as conceived objectively', nor something 'brought into existence by [personal] action'. Never mind, also, the fact that, after expending considerably energy attributing to Marxism full blame for the violent political acts committed in its namesake, Peterson appears totally unperturbed by Heidegger's direct involvement with the Nazi regime. For what's interesting here, if we truck with reading Peterson's pedestrian reading for a moment, is the way that—while Peterson seems to believe there exists a compatibility between his own Jungian-influenced stress on the need for 'belief' and the work of Heidegger—this conceit ignores a crucial aspect of Heidegger's work. For Heidegger, who was deeply influenced by Nietzsche, Christian metaphysics was guilty of *Seinsvergessenheit* ('forgetfulness of being')[20]—it, in other words, discourages the relationship to finitude, to temporality, necessary to render Being authentic (while Being is not brought into existence by personal action, for Heidegger, it can be rendered authentic through it). For Peterson, by contrast, individuals are not free to *'invent our own values'* in this way. This is because, apropos our biology, *'we cannot merely impose what we believe on our souls'*.

Or can we? If Peterson and Derrida share certain features in common, it's partly because they both come from a similar historical context: the so-called 'postmodern' era, in which, as Lyotard observed, knowledge has become so catalogued and commercialized so as to lose its sacral character (*ergo*, Peterson and Derrida's shared allergy to 'metanarratives' such as Marxism). And the fact that even Peterson cannot escape this historical matrix should clue us into the deep absurdity of his accusation that Derrida was the 'leader' of a group of 'postmodernists' who singularly conspired to create it. Certainly, Derrida was by no means naïve regarding the extent to which he was the product of history (though he sometimes over stresses the extent to which this history, this 'rupture', was *intellectual* in origin). In his interview with Sprinker, for instance, Derrida claims that he 'burst out laughing' when he heard that he and Foucault had been accused of being responsible for the US Senate's 1987 blocking of Judge Robert Bork to the Supreme Court[21], due to the 'destabilize[ing]' effect of their ideas on questions regarding the 'original intent' of the Constitution. Deconstruction, he points out bemusedly, was not the 'cause' of Bork's failure. Rather, deconstruction *itself* emerged due to a more 'general deconstruction' that was already taking place at the level of society—a 'general deconstruction' which, he admits, it likely helped nurture.

Even if Derrida and Peterson both respond to the same problematic, however, they both represent decidedly different ways of dealing with it. Derrida, while aware that the sciences could only be superadded to, not supplanted, by deconstruction, never resigned himself to the notion that logocentrism was an inexorable consequence of our biological makeup (a gesture Catherine Malabou has admirably carried forth with her investigations of the way that 'plasticity' is intrinsic to our neurobiological functioning). In this way, he remained a defender of the rationalizing legacy of the Enlightenment—even if the defence of this legacy paradoxically required undermining many of its presuppositions. Peterson's vision is, in a sense, far bleaker, involving as it does the time-honoured reactionary gesture of assigning limits to what reason, or the zeal for equality, can achieve—limits that he justifies through a bizarre farrago of psychological writings old and new. In *12 Rules for Life*, Peterson, with trademark apocalyptic flare, declares that: 'It is almost impossible to over-estimate the nihilistic and destructive nature of [Derrida's] philosophy'; a philosophy which 'puts the act of categorization itself in doubt'. But all of this raises the question: who's really the nihilist—the man who proposes we change the way we think reality? Or the man who claims it can't be done?

Chapter Nine

The Rebate of the Century, OR How Žižek Could've DESTROYED Peterson

When things break down, what has been ignored rushes in.
Jordan Peterson, 12 Rules for Life

The Great Debate: Origin and Structure

On 17 December 2018, Jordan Peterson issued a starkly worded invitation to the world's most well-known Marxist philosopher. 'Any time, any place, Mr Žižek,' he wrote in a tweet, which contained attached images of himself, Žižek and—lest you doubt Peterson's ability to hold his own against an esteemed thinker—previous interlocutor Steven Pinker. And in spite of seeming more like a challenge to a street brawl than a debate—a philosophy discussion would presumably take place in an auditorium, probably somewhere between 6 and 10pm—it was quickly discerned that Peterson's intention was, indeed, to challenge Slavoj Žižek, the 'Elvis of cultural theory', to the latter.

The provocation in question concerned Žižek's appearance, just over 5 weeks earlier, at Cambridge Union Society. There, Žižek—when asked by the moderator whether he agreed with Peterson's opinion that it would be good for the US Democratic Party to, in the moderator's paraphrase, 'get badly beaten in the midterms' to 'give them a kick up the ass'—briefly offered a reiteration of his previously taken stance that Trump's election affords the opportunity to create 'a new consensus'. But then, something else happened. Žižek, digressing from the question, began to give his opinions on Peterson *as an intellectual*. 'With all his pseudo-scientific references, you know, he cannot talk about women and marriage without discussing lobsters...', he mocked, noting that any effort to model human behaviour upon that of animals is 'madness' due to the 'unnatural' character of notions like equality and freedom. His next comments were even more blistering: Peterson's attempt to dispense Jungian-inspired 'wisdom', Žižek argued, represents the antithesis of the Christian and Greek philosophic traditions, which oppose 'holism' and circularity in favour of 'social disruption'. 'Here I react like Goebbels,' Žižek joked of his attitude towards thinkers who advise on the best means of restoring 'balance' to one's life. 'I reach for my gun.'

In fact, this wasn't the first time Peterson had tried to challenge Žižek to a debate. In early 2018, after the publication of an article by Žižek in *The Independent* that claimed Peterson's popularity reflected the incapacity of the Left to adequately criticize the mistruths promulgated via 'the PC universe of obsessive regulation', Peterson tweeted that: 'If you wish to debate the validity of my "apparently" scientific theories—or any of my other claims, then let me know, and we'll arrange it...' The only problem was *who* he'd tweeted it to: a faux-Žižek quotes account; one not manned by the social media adverse Slovenian himself but by a fan. But a video released on Peterson's official YouTube channel on 28 February 2019 confirmed that this time the debate would, indeed, take place—specifically, in Toronto, on 19 April. What followed was a row of public excitement that—if not unseen in the history of philosophy—was the first of its type in the twenty-first century, when the existence of the Internet and heightened levels of university enrolment had allowed for the respective cults of thinkers like Žižek and Peterson to englobe much of the youth worldwide. 'The debate of the century,' it was dubbed by journalists. T-shirts were hocked by independent vendors online, with the mugs of Žižek and Peterson and the words 'Team Žižek' and 'Team Peterson' emblazoned on them. Scalped tickets for the 3000-seat Sony Centre were running at higher prices than tickets for the Toronto Maple Leafs-Boston Bruins NHL playoff game set to take place the same day (and this is *Canada*). Meanwhile, behind the scenes, Peterson and his people were scrambling to exert as much control over the event as they could before the 19 April deadline. The debate would take place on Peterson's home turf[22]. But in addition, Stephen Blackwood—the founding president of Ralston College, an avowedly anti-PC 'university' that's motto is SERMO LIBER VITA IPSA ('Free Speech Is Life Itself'), and that includes Peterson among its board of visitors—was selected by them to moderate, on the grounds that he represented a 'neutral' choice. And rather than provide a free livestream, as per Žižek's request, Peterson's claque elected to charge for it, pocketing all the proceeds for themselves (though Žižek did succeed in getting its cost down to 15 dollars a pop). Somewhere in the midst of all this, Žižek, perhaps wanting to distance himself from the transparent profit-taking going on, announced that he'd be donating his speaking fee from the event to charity[23].

Given the hoopla that preceded the event, it would've been difficult for Žižek and Peterson—after taking to the stage nearly half an hour late—to live up to expectations. They didn't. The debate, which was titled 'Happiness: Capitalism vs. Marxism' ostensibly centred around the question of which system is better poised to engender global bliss. In practice, however, much of it involved Žižek reading off prefab talking points from a prepared script while an intellectually underpowered Peterson frantically attempted to keep pace with the complexity of his monologue. Part of this was inevitable: for all of the disdain he directs at 'affirmative action', Peterson is, in his own way, a product of it—no one but a right-wing philosopher with his level of media support, after all, could've parlayed a threat to misgender his students and a self-help book peppered with Nietzsche references into an opportunity to debate with arguably the world's most esteemed cultural theorist. But part of it was also by design. For rather than, in the infantile parlance of the alt-right, trying to 'DESTROY' Peterson, Žižek clearly took it upon himself to refocus the debate from its confrontational premise to an exploration of the things he and Peterson *share in common*—among them a disdain for political correctness and an appreciation of the role that belief plays in structuring political discourse.

This is a wholly defensible strategy: Žižek clearly understood that the hoped-for slugfest, were it to transpire, could only have the effect of reaffirming the audience's existing presuppositions; of widening the existing ideological chasm between left and right. By refusing to try to deliver a knockout blow then, he succeeded in both wooing Peterson's fan base—of disabusing them of the notion that one must necessarily be right-wing in order to oppose left-liberal political correctness—as well as rejecting the more agonistic model of verbal sparring they characteristically prefer. One consequence of this approach, however, is that many of Peterson's factually dubious remarks went unanswered throughout the debate. This includes Peterson's opening salvo, in which he unsuccessfully attempted, by laying out and critiquing 'ten of the fundamental axioms' of *The Communist Manifesto*, to lure Žižek into a more pedantic discussion regarding the pros and cons of said text. In honour of this gesture, then, this section of the book will conclude with a point-by-point response to Peterson's ten critiques. As Peterson clearly intends these critiques to redouble as a dismissal of Marx's philosophy *tout court*—and as he expressly cites terms throughout his argument that do not derive from *The Communist Manifesto*—it seems appropriate to draw from the entirety of Marx and Engels' oeuvre in responding:

Proposition 1: History is to be viewed primarily as an economic class struggle

After a brief prelude in which Peterson claims that, in *The Communist Manifesto*, Marx and Engels failed to interrogate their own presuppositions, or to 'think about thinking'—a remark that ignores both the degree to which the duo were steeped in dialectics, as well as the fact that *The Communist Manifesto* is, at bottom, a zippy political pamphlet—Peterson gets down to his first point. This is that, while *The Communist Manifesto* sees history as conceptualizable through an 'economic lens', in reality there are 'many other motivations that drive humans' such as, for instance, 'economic cooperation'.

Neither the claim that history is defined by economic class struggle or, in Peterson's highly scientific parlance, 'other motivations' are, obviously, falsifiable—though one could quite reasonably follow the path of Althusser here in denoting that historical materialism is *scientifically*, rather than *philosophically*, demonstrable. It's for this reason, perhaps, that Engels—after Marx's death—attempted to elucidate the relationship of 'base' (the means of production) and 'superstructure' (culture/ ideology). We cite here two signal examples. In his 1884 text *The Origin of the Family, Private Property, and the State*, Engels argues that the 'materialist conception' of history involves the two-fold recognition of 1) the production of material objects, and 2) the reproduction of humans (e.g. the family)—a move that opens the door to understanding the 'ties of kinship' that dominate pre-agricultural societies as akin to a mode of production. And in his famed 1890 letter to Joseph Bloch, Engels states that—while he and Marx felt compelled to assert the importance of economic determinacy to combat 'our adversaries, who denied it'—it is by no means 'the *only*' determining element of history, with the superstructure also playing an important role.

The question of the suitability of the materialist schema for understanding history is then, as can probably be gleaned from the above, a legitimate conundrum (and indeed, the 'postmodern' era has been defined partially by a rejection of it). Stranger is Peterson's claim that Marx does not recognize the significance of 'economic cooperation' as a historical motivation. For Marx, 'co-operation' has always been integral to human life.

Indeed, it is the particularly co-operative and uniform character of industrial production—in which 'the subjective principle of the division of labour no longer exists' due to advancements in automation—that, in part, furnishes the conditions for mass proletarian organization...

Proposition 2: Marx believes that all hierarchical structures exist because of capitalism

According to Peterson, Marx espouses the view, in *The Communist Manifesto*, that all hierarchies exist due to capitalism—something Peterson disagrees with, citing evidence that human hierarchies stretch into 'Paleolithic times', even predating 'human history itself'. However, Marx never says that all hierarchy owes to capitalism, in *The Communist Manifesto* or elsewhere. In the Paris manuscripts, for instance, Marx writes that the entrenchment of money as the 'universal commodity' results in a situation where:

...what I am and what I can do is by no means determined by my individuality. I am ugly, but I can buy the most beautiful woman. Which means to say that I am not ugly, for the effect of ugliness, its repelling power, is destroyed by money. As an individual, I am lame, but money procures me 24 legs. Consequently, I am not lame. I am a wicked, dishonest, unscrupulous and stupid individual, but money is respected, and so also is its owner. Money is the highest good, and consequently its owner is also good. Moreover, money spares me the trouble of being dishonest, and I am therefore presumed to be honest. I am mindless, but if money is the true mind of all things, how can its owner be mindless? What is more, he can buy clever people for himself, and is not he who has power over clever people cleverer than them? Through money, I can have anything the human heart desires. Do I not possess all human abilities? Does not money therefore transform all my incapacities into their opposite?

On this account, it is the development of commodity-producing society that is responsible for the perversion of 'natural' (if not necessarily strictly *biological*) hierarchies!

Proposition 3: Marx doesn't acknowledge the existence of nature

Marx, for Peterson, commits an egregious blunder in *The Communist Manifesto* by failing to recognize the 'primary conflict' that defines human societies—the way we are perennially at 'odds with nature'.

The word 'nature' is used just twice in *The Communist Manifesto* to refer to the natural world. The first instance of this—when Marx characterizes capitalism as having achieved the 'Subjection of nature's forces by man'—gives a good indication of his stance towards man's relationship to nature in this period: essentially, that while it *once* served as an obstacle, the technological gains made by capitalism have since endowed us with the ability to overcome the limitations it imposes (so call Peterson half-right).

For a long time, this naïve position—which Marx applies to critique Malthus' theory of population growth, arguing that Juston von Leibig's 'soil science' demonstrates that food supply growth can be exponential, and that soil degradation can be warded off indefinitely—was accepted as the only one derivable from his scientific works. More recently, however, Marxist scholars have challenged this. Kohei Saito, for instance, in his 2018 text *Karl Marx's Ecosocialism*, shows how—beginning in the 1860s, in response to the waning of Leibig's optimism regarding the use of synthetic fertilizers to reverse soil degradation—Marx moderates his position on the ability of humans to outstrip nature.

Proposition 4: Marx believes history can be conceived as a binary class struggle between the proletariat and the bourgeoisie

This is not correct. While Marx does claim that class struggle is the basis of all 'hitherto existing societies' in *The Communist Manifesto*—a claim that he would later soften due to his study of the anthropological works of Lewis Henry Morgan—he *does not* suggest that the conflict between the bourgeoisie and proletariat is transhistorical. This is quite clear from the *Manifesto*, where Marx claims that 'the first elements of the bourgeoisie were developed' from 'the chartered burghers of the earliest towns' of the Middle Ages. Peterson, then, is confusing two things: the way that capitalism, according to Marx, 'simplified class antagonisms' where it sprung up, dividing society increasingly into bourgeoisie and proletariat, and the transhistorical nature of 'class struggle'.

Peterson's attempt to link this oversight—Marx's supposed failure to identify classes other than the bourgeoisie and proletariat—to the liquidation of the kulaks in Soviet Russia is particularly puzzling. In *The Communist Manifesto*, Marx expressly acknowledges 'peasants' such as the kulaks, classifying them as members of the 'middle class' who are 'not revolutionary, but conservative' (though he also states that there is no point in abolishing their property where they possess it, as industrialization is already hastening its demise).

Proposition 5: Marx assumes that all good is on the side of the proletariat and all the evil is on the side of the bourgeoisie

While Marx does romanticize the proletariat, this romanticism is intimately connected, particularly from the mid-1840s onward, with his understanding of the economic role that it plays within society. As he writes in the preface to the German edition of the first volume of *Capital*:

...here individuals are dealt with only in so far as they are the personifications of economic categories, embodiments of particular class-relations and class-interests. My standpoint, from which the evolution of the economic formation of society is viewed as a process of natural history, can less than any other make the individual responsible for relations whose creature he socially remains, however much he may subjectively raise himself above them.

It's for this reason that Marx lauds the bourgeois as the revolutionary class crucial to the shift from feudalism to capitalism—a role the proletariat, in its struggle for communism, has since inherited. Subjective conceptions of morality may befit a bourgeois society, given the contradiction between its delegation of individual rights and the failure of them to manifest on the terrain of social reality. But Marx's approach to morality represents a radicalization of what Hegel describes, in the *Phenomenology of Spirit*, as the synthesis of ethical life [*Sittlichkeit*] characteristic of the state, in which the individual will is understood as inextricable from consciousness of universality (and thus, with a little bit of dialectical nudging, inextricable from the spirit of world history, or *Weltgeist*).

Proposition 6: That the dictatorship of the proletariat must be brought about as the first stage of communist revolution

The term 'dictatorship of the proletariat' is not used in *The Communist Manifesto*. In fact, it wouldn't appear in Marx's writings until 4 years *after* the *Manifesto*'s publication, due to its usage in an article by communist journalist Joseph Weydemeyer (though Marx did use similar phrases prior to this—'rule of the proletariat', for instance). Moreover, while Marx, in his 1852 correspondence with Weydemeyer, states that 'the class struggle necessarily leads to the dictatorship of the proletariat', he later, in an 1872 speech, declared that there are nations—such as America, England and Holland—'where the workers can attain their goal by peaceful means'. This *seeming* contradiction attests to the fact the term 'dictatorship' had not yet acquired, when Marx wrote, its present-day association with draconian top-down rule. The Paris Commune, for instance, which he described as 'a proletarian *dictature*', was, in Marx's words: 'Formed of the municipal councilors, chosen by universal suffrage in the various wards of the town, responsible, and revocable at short terms. The majority of its members were naturally workers, or acknowledged representatives of the working class. The Commune was to be a working, not a parliamentary body, executive, and legislative at the same time.'

The stress Marx lays here on the importance of direct democracy to the revolutionary commune reflects his own awareness of one of the objections to his thought that Peterson cites—namely, that members of the proletariat elevated to significant positions wouldn't be corrupted by their acquisition of 'sudden access to power' (in 1875, for instance, Marx wrote that a workers' state would likely suffer certain 'defects' due to being 'economically, morally and intellectually...still stamped with the birth marks of the old society from whose womb it emerges'). In this respect, Marx's use of the term 'dictatorship of the proletariat' differs from the subsequent Blanqui-influenced, putschist definition given to it by Plekhanov—a definition that would, later, come to influence Lenin[24].

Proposition 7: Nothing that capitalists do constitutes valid labour

Peterson's use of the term 'valid' here to characterize Marx's position is highly misleading. For Marx, the distinction between 'productive' or 'unproductive' labour is not a normative judgement but one that reflects the logic of capital. A labourer is productive if they generate surplus value; they are unproductive if they do not. Thus, for Marx, 'a schoolmaster is a productive labourer when, in addition to belabouring the heads of his scholars, he works like a horse to enrich the school proprietor'. By this criteria, a teacher employed by the state— regardless of the importance of their role in enhancing the value of labour power—is not a productive labourer. And ironically, while the unproductive/productive originates in Adam Smith, Marx later wields it *against him*, by noting the unproductivity of the labour of the capitalist when seen from this standpoint.

Clearly, the designation of all labour that does not directly bestow surplus value to the capitalist as 'unproductive' cannot provide a complete description of the economies of twentieth-century industrial states such as the Soviet Union and the United States, dependent as they were on massive programmes of state investment targeted at heightening economic productivity. It is for this reason that many dissident Trotskyists, in particular, have—in large part as a means of critiquing the USSR—adopted the term 'state capitalism' to refer to the process whereby a state acts as a corporation, extracting surplus value from the workforce and investing it in production (Trotsky himself maintained that the USSR was a degenerated workers' state). To assume, however, that Marx's theory has simply been outmoded by the economic changes inaugurated over the course of the past century is unfair to it. Moishe Postone, for instance, argues in his 1993 text *Time, Labour, and Social Domination* that 'traditional Marxists' have often failed to understand that Marx's critique in *Capital* is 'immanent', in the sense that capital is analysed *from its own standpoint* (assuming that the 'labour theory of value' holds transhistorically, for instance, as opposed to being a consequence of the historical generalization of the law of value). Similarly, it is easy to observe that the distinction Marx makes between 'productive' and 'unproductive' labour is intended to performatively illustrate the contradictions inherent within capitalism—not to furnish us with a ready-at-hand criteria to base communism upon.

Proposition 8: Profit is theft

Ironically, Peterson's formulation of Marx's position on profit—that he believed 'profit is theft'—appears not to channel Marx, but the French politician and anarchist Pierre-Joseph Proudhon, who coined the slogan 'property is theft' in 1840. Marx was, as a competitor for the attentions of the Left who found Proudhon intellectually vacuous, not a fan. 'Theft' as a forcible violation of property presupposes the existence of property, he wrote of this catchphrase in 1865, caustically adding that Proudhon entangles himself in 'all sorts of fantasies, obscure even to himself, about true bourgeois property'.

This dispute aside, Marx clearly *did* think that the appropriation of the surplus value created by workers—the basis of profit—was exploitative. In this respect, he differs from Peterson, who argues that 1) the profits accrued by capitalists frequently represent 'fair' remuneration for their labour, 2) that profit is necessary to furnish capitalists with 'security', 3) that profits permit enterprises to expand, and 4) that the profit motive helps safeguard against the wastage of labour.

We'll respond to these points summarily:

1. Peterson here reprises an old trope of classical political economy—the idea that the capitalist's 'profits of stock' are tantamount to what Smith characterizes as wages for 'the labour of inspection and direction'. Yet what Marx shows, through a careful dissection of Smith's work in *Theories of Surplus-Value*, is that Smith 'wrongly presents capital and land as independent sources of exchange-value' and that to render his theories internally consistent one must acknowledge that 'labour is...the only source of value, and the price of wages and the price of profits arise out of this source of value'. This does not mean, of

course, that Steve Jobs didn't add value to Apple—in so far as he also *worked* for the company, he was responsible for the creation of value (and *a lot* it, we can presume). But the bulk of his wealth, coming as it did from his 'profits of stock', was not a *wage*, nor remuneration for 'his' labour.

2. Profits may, indeed, furnish capitalists with 'security'. But in so far as they exist on account of the extraction of surplus value, they also deprive workers of it. Moreover, given the inextricability of capitalism from the boom and bust cycle—which occurs (to offer a highly simplified formulation) due to the tendency of capitalism to proportionally skew towards investment in automation, before having to reboot itself—even capitalists may not be as secure as they'd like.

3. It's true that, by profit-taking, capitalists are able to make further outlays in productive investment, thereby growing their capital. But productive investment itself is by no means dependent on the enrichment of the capitalist through the exploitation of surplus value. In his polemic against Lassalle in the *Critique of the Gotha Programme*, for instance, Marx states that even under socialism, workers will never receive the 'undiminished' proceeds of their labour due to the need for reinvestment in, among other things, 'the general costs of administration not belonging to production'.

4. The term 'waste' is underspecified by Peterson. It is often assumed, for instance, that public-sector employees are 'overpaid' due to the fact they (typically) receive a higher proportion of the value they create than private-sector ones (and notwithstanding the difficulties that often arise in calculating this). But such a judgement already belies the axiomatic assumption that *capitalists are entitled to surplus value*. To say this, however, is to

not go far enough in the critique of value as a regulative norm. Public-sector employees exist partly due to the fact that the capitalist category of 'productive labour' does not suffice to meet the need of *capitalism*, let alone society (nations where medicare is private, for instance, tend to pay *more* for it—a cost capitalists must also bear, in the form of the provision of private insurance). Such contradictions are observable everywhere. It is likely more socioeconomically contributive, for instance, for an unemployed PhD graduate to stay at home and write Wikipedia articles than for him/her to flip burgers at McDonald's, pricing themselves below the cost of automation. Due to the diktats of capital, though, they cannot do this—and thus must 'waste' their labour power on a job that offers less to society!

Proposition 9: The dictatorship of the proletariat will become magically productive

The term 'dictatorship of the proletariat', as mentioned before, does not appear in *The Communist Manifesto*. Nor was it applied by Marx, as Peterson suggests, to refer to a state of 'absurd centralization'. But to respond to Peterson's main point here, there are good reasons to think that communism, if implemented on a global scale, could be more productive than capitalism. Faced—as they regularly are—with an onslaught of automative breakthroughs that in turn render large swaths of workers redundant, capitalists normally follow a two-pronged strategy, phasing out a significant proportion of their workforce while nevertheless retaining more workers than would be strictly necessary from the standpoint of production in order to buoy their derivation of profit from surplus value (a move that depresses productive efficiency in so far as it *forestalls* the implementation of automation). Eventually, this results in a situation where demand is spavined vis-à-vis supply, due to the fact workers who are unemployed (or underemployed) cannot *buy up the supply of goods on the market.* This leads to recession— or depression[25]. At this point, one of two things transpires: (1) the government steps in, redistributing wealth in order to subsidize demand, or (2) a massive 'cleaning' takes place through which excess supply—and with it, capital—is destroyed (war can also be efficient for this end). In practice, in the twentieth century, *both* of these remedies have been necessary, with the ballooning of the size of state apparatuses owing largely to the need to offset the diminution in demand caused by developments in automation.

This model is, of course, highly skeletal, and subject to variation depending on the context in which it manifests. From 1979-2007, for instance, the US economy managed to stave off extensive destruction of capital and/or wealth redistribution by extending consumer credit in its stead—consumer credit that was in turn used to buy goods manufactured in the Third World, where labour costs were below the costs of domestic automation. That this strategy eventually backfired demonstrates the inextricability of the boom and bust cycle to capitalism. And therein lies the chief economic advantage of communism. For by emancipating itself from the injunction to produce surplus value—by, in other words, making the workers the direct beneficiaries of the productive gains of industry—communism would be able to avert the diminution of demand, thereby putting an end to man-made recessionary cycles (as well as abolishing the current disincentive to deploy automation—namely, the fact that profit is dependent on surplus value extraction).

Of course, all of this raises the question of logistics—how would such a society be organized? While this is too complex a question to get into here, we should note that Peterson's reference to the 'impossible computation' required to complete this task is provocative, given that many Marxists—Nick Srnicek, for instance—have suggested that computation has now obtained a level of sophistication that would permit it to do just that. This is not a wholly new idea: from 1971-73, to cite a prominent example, Chilean Marxist president Salvador Allende oversaw 'Project Cybersyn', which sought to create a computational decision support system to aid in the planning of a socialist economy (before being overthrown in a bloody US-backed military coup).

Proposition 10: Marx and Engels admit that capitalism is the most productive system of production ever, yet still wish to overthrow it

It's true, certainly, that Marx and Engels acknowledged the huge productive strides that had been made under capitalism — and it's for this reason that their vision of 'scientific socialism' amounts to a synthesis, not *determinate negation*, of its structure. Peterson, however, enmeshes himself here in contradiction. For if capitalism is already creating 'material security' for 'everyone' at a rate that is 'unparalleled in human history' this is not due to capitalism *per se* but rather due to the pressure exerted by the masses to redistribute its productive gains. Paradoxically, these efforts have allowed capitalism to—in altered form—survive, by tempering its tendency towards iniquitous distribution, thereby staving off the threat of revolution.

Today, however—in a world where corporate profits are easily stashed in Bahamian text shelters, and labour costs are undercut by hiring up Third-World workers to sew up soccer balls behind barbed wire—capitalism appears to be on the cusp of abolishing its own conditions of existence. Thus the consequences of its unfettered application become apparent: ceaseless recession, and an increasing disparity between rich and poor. Should this drift persist, the question of whether reform or revolution will be needed to remedy it will become purely academic. For the structural change required to make capitalism viable—as we enter an age of self-driving taxis and robotized caregivers—

will, even if pursued under the watchword of reform, need to *be* revolutionary in its redistributive aspiration.

Conclusion: Buying and Selling Ideology

We leave you with one final thought. Peterson, after describing the enrichment that's supposedly transpired due to capitalism, states that, in light of this, it makes sense to 'let the system play itself out'. Though he adds a caveat: unless, that is, 'you're assuming that the evil capitalists are just gonna take all of the flat screen televisions and put them in one big room'. Today, the world's 26 richest people control the same amount of wealth as the 3.8 billion poorest[26]. That's *half* the world's population. Spare me the maths: just how many flat screen televisions could that buy?

Part III

Peterson on Feminism and Reason:
By Marion Trejo and Ben Burgis

On Peterson's Anti-Feminism:
By Marion Trejo

Introduction

In this brief chapter I discuss Peterson's anti-feminism. Although on more than one occasion his insensible and grandiose statements resulted in him arguing he is not in fact an anti-feminist, I argue that this disposition actually runs deep. It is prominently displayed in what I call the four contradictions in Peterson's approach to feminism: the use of radical feminism as a synecdoche for feminism generally, the mischaracterization of patriarchy as tyranny, the misrepresentation of gender equality and the use of natural hierarchies to justify gender differences, and the recourse to a male victimization narrative to displace women's issues. Despite some animosity from the left when engaging with Peterson, this book's authors contend that he must be argued against rigorously when providing a critique. In this spirit, I name these contradictions precisely because once his arguments are examined it becomes evident that Peterson holds inconsistent ideas regarding feminism.

The Use of Radical Feminism as a Synecdoche for Feminism

In the *Q&A* Australian television discussion programme Peterson stated that he is not 'an anti-feminist per se' because he believes in the integration of both men and women into the workforce. However, Peterson continues, he is against 'a brand of more radical feminism that insists that our culture is best characterized as an oppressive patriarchy'. Superficially this appears to be Peterson's final and public position; not as antagonistic to feminism but as the voice of reason calling out the extreme radicalism of a certain type of feminism. Although he has repeatedly voiced his disagreement with radical feminists influencing and allegedly dominating debates in the university and politics, these concerns are mostly about issues advanced not by radical feminists in particular but by feminism more broadly speaking.

Take, for example, the gender pay gap. During his interview with Cathy Newman, Peterson argued that contrary to what 'radical feminists claim', the gender pay gap is the product of multiple causes beyond the persistence of patriarchal norms and institutions. Claiming it is only 'radical feminists' who are concerned with the gender pay gap is inaccurate. Historically one must note that the gender pay gap was an issue brought to the public attention by second-wave feminists; including many liberal feminists. These activists agitated for the fair inclusion of women into the labour force. Liberal feminists often contended with radical feminists like Simone de Beauvoir who advocated for the subversion of all forms of male-produced (and dominated) social, political and economic relations. Other concerns that Peterson wrongly attributes exclusively to radical feminism include the lack of women in Science, Technology, Engineering and Mathematics (STEM) fields or women's representation in politics and companies. Once more many liberal feminists and even conservatives like Kellyanne Conway have advocated for more women becoming involved in politics. In an abuse of rhetorical images, Peterson uses radical feminism as a synecdoche for feminism to 'mask' his hostility towards feminism and female involvement in politics generally.

This opposition is best expressed in his classification of feminism as part of the radical Left or the so-called post-modern neo-Marxists identitarians. Since the problems with this overarching category were earlier discussed in this book (see Hamilton and McManus' chapters), my critique highlights the fact that this classification neglects the heterogeneity of feminism as both a movement and a theoretical approach. It is indeed true that there are radical, Marxist, post-modern and identitarian feminists. However, we can also find liberal, revolutionary, progressive, post-colonial, difference-oriented, catholic, conservative and even post-feminist feminists, among many others. Each of these groups hold different, sometimes even contradictory views. A liberal feminist like Martha Nussbaum may characterize Judith Butler as a 'Professor of Parody' while breaking with radicals like Catharine MacKinnon in her willingness to tolerate prostitution. Peterson's totalizing portrayal overlooks that most women-related issues on the policy agenda today reached this position because they are supported and advocated for by a wide array of feminists. Peterson makes generalizations about all different forms of feminist agitation on the basis of a few issues which are rarely even the subject of an overlapping consensus.

Furthermore, Peterson misrepresents feminism as a radical unified political movement whose objectives include destroying Western values and promoting hostility to men through waging a war against masculinity. This speaks of a Western-centred view that is either ignorant, unaware or simply indifferent to women's issues in the global south. Peterson universalizes localized problems in developed countries that are not representative at all about women's issues (like the *Act to amend the Canadian Human Rights Act* and the *Criminal Code* or the new guidelines for the treatment of men and boys from the *American Psychological Association*) and uses them as arguments against the need of feminism and feminist informed public policies. This slim geographical and cultural imagination disdains the many places where women's rights are nothing but formal declarations (if they exist whatsoever) of political systems that allow, either by omission or complicity, their systematic violation.

Peterson also fails to acknowledge that feminists have an uneasy, changing and relational approach to masculinity. As Judith Kegan Gardiner pointed out in the introduction to the book *Masculinity Studies and Feminist Theory: New Directions*

(2002), the 'relationships between masculinity, masculinity studies, feminism, and feminist theories are asymmetrical, interactive, and changing'. Gardiner's book includes different feminist approaches to masculinity that illustrate the complexity of this relation; from the radical ones that perceive men and masculinity as the enemies, to the poststructuralists that understand masculinity as endorsed through structures of domination, to queer and performative theories that advocate for biological de-essentialization of people, which is to say, to break away all together from sex and gender categories. In the words of Judith Lorber, there are gender reform feminisms, gender resistant feminisms and gender revolution feminisms, all of which think differently about masculinity and men.

The Mischaracterization of Patriarchy as Tyranny

In various interviews Peterson has claimed that feminism is a tyrannical and appalling movement. On the one hand, feminism is represented as a set of oppressive strategies against men, examples according to Rule 12 include trying to prevent men from being men, feminizing universities and the workplace, and pushing men towards becoming interested in 'harsh, fascist political ideology'. At the same time, feminism is critiqued by its portrayal of society as patriarchal. These are separate claims that too often are framed by Peterson as similar arguments; we are going to dissect them starting with the latter.

Peterson takes on feminism for depicting our societies as oppressive patriarchies. In *12 Rules for Life*, although he doesn't explicitly mention feminism, referring instead to ideologies and radical leftists indoctrinating students in the university, he belittles those who think 'culture is an oppressive structure' in which men tyrannize women.

As a feminist concept, patriarchy was introduced by second-wave feminism to unify the political struggle and to provide a theoretical framework that explained women's role in society.

This, however, doesn't mean that there is a unified feminist definition of patriarchy, as Peterson often implies. In *Sexual Politics* (1969), Kate Millett wrote that patriarchy is a system of male domination over females. Patriarchy refers to any 'power-structured relationship', 'institution' or 'arrangement' through which men dominate women. She highlights the role of family as the fundamental unit of patriarchy that socializes children into sexually differentiated roles. For Shulamith Firestone (*The Dialectic of Sex*, 1971), patriarchy refers to men's oppression, specifically to the control of women's reproductive capabilities. Finella McKenzie made a similar argument emphasizing how women's biology is also transformed into psychological dependency. Most second-wave feminists refer to concrete patriarchal forms, either the oppressive gender differentiations (re)produced first in the family or men's control over women's reproductive capacities (remember the slogan 'the personal is political'). In addition to second-wave feminism, Marxist feminism claims that women are members of a class exploited by global and national capitalist elites who are mostly men, and critical race theory, as formulated by Kimberlé Williams Crenshaw, explains how subordination, marginalization, domination and exploitation are experienced differently according to the diverse intersecting categories that cannot be limited to gender. What I argue here is that regardless of the approach we are looking at, feminism rarely characterizes society as mere tyrannical domination (to my recollection only Mary Wollstonecraft spoke, in *A Vindication of the Rights of Woman* (1792), of 'the tyranny of men'). Tyranny might be a rhetorical figure of radical feminism but not an accepted theoretical concept. Any knowledgeable person in political theory distinguishes tyranny as a system of government from patriarchy, a social structure that exceeds the compounds of the government's apparatuses.

Second, the concept of patriarchy cannot be rebutted by listing four men (in *12 Rules for Life* Peterson mentions Arunachalam

Muruganantham, James Young Simpson, Dr Cleveland Haas and Gregory Goodwin Pincus) whose inventions helped improve women's reproductive health. Patriarchy is a system that produces oppressive and subordinated men, and that exists even if few men aren't oppressors. The former element, presented by Millett's analysis, is one of the most ignored by anti-feminists. In Mexico, for instance, a considerable amount of social media anti-feminists would have no trouble agreeing with Peterson in blaming feminism for violence exercised over men.

Third, as Žižek pointed out in the introduction, 'the problem with [Peterson] does not reside in his lies but in the partial truths that sustain his lies'. Which is to say, Peterson might be right in stating that radical feminism definition of patriarchy highlights, according to Judith Lorber, 'men's pervasive oppression and exploitation of women, which can be found wherever women and men are in contact with each other, in private as well as in public'. Indeed there are several branches of feminism whose views on patriarchy are equally radical and problematic (examples include Catharine MacKinnon's portrayal of women as exclusively the victims of men or Andrea Dworkin's 'primal paternal rape'); however, as pointed out in the first contradiction, this doesn't mean that all forms of feminism support these theses. Finally, if we define patriarchy as 'a social structure that is male-centred, male-identified, [and] male-dominated' (Becker, 1999) there is plenty of 'hard evidence' worldwide (not limited to North America or the West) to support its existence, from the lack of women's political representation to the absence of lawful abortion on request.

Although is mostly speculation given Peterson's lack of clarity (thus violating his own rule), I think his motivations when characterizing patriarchy as tyrannical are two-fold. First, if patriarchy only exists when it is tyrannical then there is no patriarchy at all in the West since none of its forms of government are tyrannical (the question about the rest, non-Western world, remains open, though). Consequentially, feminists are wrong and feminism is irrelevant. Second, Peterson wants to expose but mostly misrepresent feminists. In the podcast with Anne McElvoy, he claimed that patriarchy is a 'story founded in resentment'. I agree but not for the same reasons. In Mexico, where women's lives are expendable, as we are in so many parts of the globe, resentment can be understandable. This is not to say that it is justifiable. As Peterson, I also believe that resentment is dangerous; however, unlike Peterson who wishes to treat the psychological causes by taking individual responsibility, I think resentment is a symptom of all that is wrong in our societies that cannot be reduced to individualized problems. Overcoming individual resentment doesn't exclude overcoming its political causes as Peterson falsely dichotomizes. Some feminists might be angry, yes, but it is incorrect to generalize feminists as hateful, guilt-driven individuals that advocate for abandoning personal responsibility in the face of systemic issues. Peterson overlooks that most feminists take the problem of agency seriously by asking what women can do regardless of the systems of domination in which we are embedded: political feminism is precisely the practical answer to that question.

Peterson also decries patriarchy because it dangerously divides society in identity, PC-driven groups that target men as the enemy. Let's be clear: Peterson's strategy here is to express disapproval by pointing out a limitation of identity feminism (defending womanhood as the core of the feminist struggle has been an issue criticized by numerous feminists, Judith Butler included, for example). Yet, it is bordering on to absurd to frame demands for equality before the law, respect, the right to live violence and exploitation free, and the right to be addressed by one's preferred pronoun with a tyrannical, almost totalitarian, desire to remake man and woman or with 'the longing to restructure the human spirit in the very image' of the feminist's preconceptions. If Peterson's uneasiness is with how identity-oriented feminism can become a discipline instead of an emancipatory movement he never makes this more nuanced and even valid claim. Additionally, if his issue is with the impossibility of assigning individual responsibility under a certain type of feminism which frames women as inevitable victims, he also fails to provide specific criticism.

So, in the end, the paradox relies on whether we are self-described victims invoking patriarchy as a way of displacing our incompetence or totalitarian overpowering feminists. Which one is it then?

The Misrepresentation of Gender Equality and the Use of Natural Order to Justify Gender Differences

Peterson's hollower arguments against the existence of oppressive patriarchal societies rely on the discussion of equality and natural hierarchies (yes, the lobster issue cannot be avoided). As addressed comprehensively in the book, by naturalizing existing hierarchies, Peterson roots gender differences in biological factors and uses his performance as evolutionary biology expert to make these appear not as depoliticizing statements but as fact-based assumptions based on the 'over-whelming, multi-disciplinary scientific literature'. Sadly, this is not as objectively simple as Peterson wants us to believe. In reality, there is little consensus among the scientific community, not to say in the social sciences departments, about the correlations and causal connections of sex and gender differences. Despite this debate (which certainly is irrelevant in the sense that we are no evolutionary biology experts) and granting Peterson that gender differences are built in biological elements (a view shared by some feminists), one cannot claim that any naturally produced hierarchy is justifiable, nor that we shouldn't use other resources available to us to rectify unjust hierarchies. As the Ancient Greeks pointed out long ago, we exist socially and politically by convention to remedy the arbitrariness of nature. This is why we have laws and political organizations. Even if our social hierarchies were given by nature that doesn't mean we shouldn't improve them; for instance, no scientific discovery would have been possible if humanity hadn't expanded the limits imposed on us by nature.

By stating that gender differences are natural, Peterson makes hierarchies unquestionable and inequality a justifiable state of affairs: if inequality is by nature then no one is entitled nor morally justified to ameliorate it. Since Rule 12 tells us to be wary of people that provide single cause explanations, we are going to distrust Peterson in this point too. As explained elsewhere by my co-authors, inequality is not the mere product of natural hierarchies. Inequality has socio-political and economic causes that are never systematically explored by Peterson. To him any form of social justice is driven by guilt and resentment, and any perceived sense of injustice is false consciousness or error to identify the natural sources of inequality. This is exemplified when Peterson makes the case against patriarchy by pointing to the fact that, regardless of their gender, most people living in the nineteenth century were poor (living with less than 1.2 USD) and oppressed by nature; therefore, stating that men and women were unequal is wrong. This simplistic account displaces the gender issue to one about income poverty and leaves family dynamics, which can oppress women regardless of poverty, out of the picture. Peterson plays with the fact that poor men didn't enjoy the same status or have the same opportunities as rich men to displace attention from other relevant facts, such as that poor men dominated women or that politics, economics and the legal system were male-centred and male-dominated.

This simplistic account is displayed again when he discusses the gender pay gap. Peterson argues that if the gap persists, it is not because of gender disparity but as the consequence of multiple factors mostly rooted in natural differences that make men receive more money for taking on jobs that either require more competence or because they are the only ones able to do em. What Peterson fails to recognize is that most analysts accept the multi-causality explanation while still acknowledging that gender stereotypes and social norms are substantially responsible for the gap (like the European Commission and UN Women reports). This means that even if the explanation is multi-faceted that doesn't make the gender issue less relevant or non-important. Additionally, there is also a controlled gender pay gap measure in which the differentiating elements are reduced (age, type of work, qualifications) to better reflect the gender causation. In such cases, the pay gap still persists. Finally, by drawing on the gender-equality paradox in STEM brought to public attention by Stoet and Geary (2018), Peterson argues that most of the pay gap can be explained by individual decisions. According to these authors, 'the sex differences in the magnitude of relative academic strengths and pursuit of STEM degrees rose with increases in national gender equality' with women taking on less STEM degrees than men even if they 'performed similarly to or better than boys in science in two of every three countries' analysed. These findings justify Peterson to state that, even if women are given greater equality and freedom to choose, they still do not choose degrees in fields like STEM. This ultimately impacts the jobs they take and in turn accounts for the pay difference. However, the reasons behind women's choices are still the source of plenty of debates, with people like Miller and Eagly (2015) arguing that representation of women in STEM is connected to gender stereotypes influencing women's decisions on whether to enter those fields. Additionally, there's also a lot to be said about the so-called freedom under which women around the world can choose a career or a job: globally women are more likely to live in extreme poverty (122 women per each 100 men) and girls of primary school age are less likely than boys to learn how to read (UN Women, 2018), which means their career and job opportunities are significantly reduced.

Peterson's conclusion from analysing these issues is that

the only way in which feminism deals with inequality is by attempting to eliminate gender differences; to put it simply, to feminize men and to make women more masculine. Then again this misconstrues reality, first and paradoxically because, as Peterson constantly complains, most feminisms operate on the basis of what it is to be a woman as differentiated from man, with radical feminism advocating for the elimination of any male traits from womanhood. Second, because aside from gender fluid, non-binary, or queer groups, feminism doesn't advocate for the elimination of gender differences, instead it argues against differentiation, discrimination and domination based on such differences.

By obsessively focusing on PC feminism, Peterson ignores that as an emancipatory movement, feminism wants to help women free themselves from the social, political and economic constraints imposed on us on the basis of our gender.

The Recourse to a Male Victimization Narrative to Displace Women's Issues

There is no doubt that Peterson is the gender and order guarding lobster. He frantically instructs baby lobsters not to succumb to the radical leftist dangers of the world. The lobster offers reductionist explanations and 'scientifically' coated pseudo-truths to prevent the forces of womanly chaos and post-modern neo-Marxist totalitarianism from sweeping our world into a dystopia in which everyone owns the same and *is* the same. One can correctly say that these are the utterings of a fearful, anxious and angry man but not of an alt-right man. He is still an ideologue, though, irrespective of his PR efforts to exclude himself from any ideological extremes. When it comes to the critique of feminism, he replicates the sex wars he constantly decries: men are victims of women's emancipatory achievements. And, even if the lobster guru tells both men and women to grow up and move past the undesired consequences brought by feminism, he makes sure to emphasize how men have it worse: from the decrease of men in tertiary education to the number of men in the army dying violent deaths. There is an underpinning male victim logic: men suffer because feminists altered the natural order of things. Feminism is dangerous to all, but is most dangerous to men. Herein lies Peterson's threat and brilliance; in his opaque, reactive and pseudoscientific rhetoric that easily disguises a deeply backward-looking sentiment about the role of men and women in society.

Peterson's anti-feminism is at its best and most dangerous when he attributes an 'antihuman spirit' to people that want to change the world, feminists clearly included. This antihumanism is nothing but an apocalyptic narrative to numb critical attempts to problematize society or masculinity, and is also where Peterson's reactionary disposition is more overt. This is why the Left should argue with the lobsters of the world. Peterson might not be an alt-right man as some claim but it is easy to see how he might be inspiring some.

On Lobsters, Logic and the Pitfalls of Good Rhetoric: By Ben Burgis

In 2018, University of Toronto emeritus professor of psychology Bernard Schiff published an article in *The Star* entitled, 'I was Jordan Peterson's strongest supporter. Now I think he's dangerous.'

It wasn't a very good piece. Schiff's take on his former colleague was overheated—and its effect was more to feed into than to undermine the way Peterson likes to portray himself. My friend Nathan Robinson put this point nicely in a critique in *Current Affairs*: 'Why don't I think Schiff's article is a very powerful criticism of Peterson? Because, generally speaking, I don't think calling someone a brilliant, dangerous, maverick who changes lives is a particularly good way of getting people to question them.'

Even so, Schiff's piece did provide a few interesting tidbits, like this one: 'Another thing to which I did not give sufficient concern was his teaching. As the undergraduate chair, I read all teaching reviews. His were, for the most part, excellent and included eyebrow-raising comments such as "This course has changed my life." One student, however, hated the course because he did not like "delivered truths".'

And this: 'He was preoccupied with alternative health treatments including fighting off the signs of aging as they appear on the skin, and, one time, even shamanic healing practices, where, to my great surprise and distress, he chose to be the shaman himself.'

And, most especially, this:

Several years ago, Jordan Peterson told me he wanted to buy a church…I assumed that it was for a new home—there was a trend in Toronto of converting religious spaces, vacant because of their dwindling congregations, into stylish lofts—but he corrected me. He wanted to establish a church, he said, in which he would deliver sermons every Sunday.

If you've watched any significant portion of Peterson's YouTube videos, you shouldn't have any trouble imagining what he'd be like as either a New Age shaman or an evangelical protestant preacher. He's an electrifying speaker even—maybe *especially*—when he's saying absurd things. That's why he can tell a classroom full of adults in one video that, 'although it's hard to explain', he thinks that the twinned snake imagery in ancient artwork represents the DNA Double Helix discovered in the twentieth century. There's no nervous laughter because everyone in the room is swept up in his lecture. Besides, he sounds so damn sure of himself. When he gets teary talking about (extremely poorly-defined) threats to 'the individual' in another, no one looks away in embarrassment. The reason is that, at least for people who start out with neutral or positive feelings about Peterson, the emotional intensity helps sell his message.

It's a variation of what we can think of as the Christopher Hitchens Effect. Hitchens was a great writer and a great speaker and, in his best moments, he made thoughtful and interesting points about a variety of subjects. The last years of his life, starting with his post-9/11 turn towards a particularly crude form of cheerleading for America's wars in the Middle East, were the ones in which he probably had the fewest of those 'best moments', but they were also the years in which he enjoyed the most mainstream popularity. (Conservatives liked his neocon foreign policy views. A certain kind liberal, feeling culturally besieged in George W. Bush's America, overlooked those views and loved him for his militant atheism.) A few years after the creation of YouTube in 2005, the site was full of 'Hitchslap' videos, showing the master either wittily insulting interlocutors or simply stating his abhorrence of their views with great vehemence. Many of the people who put together such videos love to talk about 'logic' or the holy trinity of 'logic, facts, and evidence', but the 'Hitchslap' clips don't really focus on Hitchens' presentation of *arguments*. They showcase someone with an accent Americans are trained to associate with intelligence forcefully stating his *conclusions*.

The Hitchens Effect works so well that a barely literate grifter like Milo Yiannopoulos was able to use it to great effect. Yiannopoulos had the accent, and he was capable of working up some half-clever sarcastic barbs, but the *content* of what he said was rarely more complicated than 'feminists are ugly bitches' or 'how can I be a racist when I love to suck black dick?' Even so, legions of American conservatives were at least temporarily taken in. So was at least one contrarian liberal. When Milo appeared on *Real Time With Bill Maher*, the host—who, remember, had invited the real Hitchens onto the show on many occasions and considered him a friend—said that Yiannopoulos reminded him 'of a young Christopher Hitchens'.

Peterson's Alberta accent and folksy language—see for example his frequent use of the word 'bucko'—are as different from the posh and boozy speech patterns of a Christopher Hitchens as a tent revival is from a debate at the Oxford Union, but he still trades on a recognizable variation of the Hitchens Effect. When someone presumed to be drawing on great reserves of knowledge speaks in a way that conveys great certainty, it's easy to feel like they're making a compelling case...even if they're actually bringing you in at the conclusion. It helps if they speak in a distinctive way. (For a particularly lazy example of this last trick, think about the way various *Star Wars* screenwriters have rearranged the syntax of Yoda's sentences at random to make his pronouncements sound more mystical and profound.) To be clear, there's nothing *wrong* with having an accent that confuses Americans—it's not the fault of any of the people I've mentioned that we tend to be rubes about that kind of thing—and there's certainly nothing wrong with packaging your arguments in the most rhetorically compelling possible way. But it's important—if you don't want to be taken in by every passing Milo—to learn how to see through the packaging and think hard about the underlying arguments.

In my Critical Thinking classes, I'll often present my students with a video clip or a quoted paragraph in which someone makes an argument and ask them to reconstruct it in 'standard form', like this:

Premise One: ....
Premise Two: ....
Premise Three: ....
Conclusion: ....

Part of the point of the exercise is that when someone is saying things you like and saying them well, it's easy to nod along without thinking too hard about how the pieces fit together. Conversely, when someone you dislike or disagree with is saying things you find annoying, it's easy to dismiss what might turn out to be a strong underlying argument. Forcing students to restate the premises in their own words helps them separate the content from its presentation and turn their attention to the question of whether those premises add up to a good reason for them to believe the conclusion.

To see how this works, let's take a representative Peterson video. It happens to be the first one I ever watched, and it addresses a subject close to my democratic socialist heart—whether the theoretical insights of Karl Marx can be separated from the horrors of twentieth-century Stalinist regimes. The video—dated 1 October 2017 and entitled 'But That Wasn't Real Communism, Socialism, or Marxism!'—starts with Peterson making his usual claim that post-modernism is just rebranded Marxism. (For an excellent discussion by Conrad Hamilton of how little substantive overlap Marx has with

Derrida, see Chapter Eight. For some of the historical specifics Peterson has to mangle to try to make this conspiratorial view of the history of philosophy work, see the Peterson chapter of Michael Brooks' book *Against the Web*.) Around the 2:25 mark he slides from denouncing post-modernism (or in Petersonian lingo, 'postmodern neo-Marxism') to mocking the idea of a form of Marxism that rejects the Soviet model: 'They certainly don't believe that they have any biological grounding, that there's any such thing as a *human being...*it's all socially constructed...which is really convenient if what you want to do is be the author of an entire socially constructed utopia that you can run...and then when the Marxists say that wasn't real Marxism, what it really means and I've thought about this for a long time, it's the most arrogant possible statement anyone could ever make, it means, "If I would have been in Stalin's position, I would have ushered in the damn utopia instead of the genocidal massacres because I understand the doctrine of Marxism and everything about me is good."' At this point (the 3:05 mark) Peterson switches to a new level of intensity in a way that almost reminds me of the turn taken by a rock song when the melodic intro ends and the guitarist and bassist start thrashing, and he says, 'Well, think again, *sunshine*, you don't understand it, you don't understand it and you're not that good and if the power was in your hands, assuming you have the competence, *which you don't*, you wouldn't have done any better, and' — speeding up now — 'if you had, there would have been someone right behind you to shoot you the first time you even tried to do anything good'.

The crowd laughs and claps at all the right points, as responsive to Peterson's rhetorical power chords as the congregation surely would have been if he'd gone ahead with his plan to buy that church in Toronto. And, as Peterson himself so often says, 'fair enough'. But let's try to reconstruct the argument. Here's an initial attempt that confines itself to the premises that Peterson has explicitly given us:

> **Premise One:** If contemporary anti-Stalinist Marxists had been leaders of a totalitarian one-party state, they would have either acted the way Stalin did or been replaced by those who would.
>
> **Premise Two:** Either way, a Stalin-like outcome would have resulted.
>
> Conclusion: ?

It seems like Peterson's implied conclusion is something sweeping like 'Marxism is inseparable from Stalinism', but that pretty clearly doesn't follow from Premises One and Two. Something that would actually follow from the premises would be:

> Conclusion: If contemporary anti-Stalinist Marxists had been leaders of a totalitarian one-party state, a Stalin-like outcome would have resulted.

If this is his conclusion, then the argument thus reconstructed is *valid*—i.e. the conclusion follows logically from the premises. As the Scottish logician Alan Weir likes to emphasize, though, logical validity both 'preserves truth upward' and 'preserves falsity downward'. In other words, if the premises of a valid argument are true, so is the conclusion (truth is preserved upward) but by the same token, if the conclusion is false, at least one of the premises must be false as well (falsity is preserved downward). An obvious objection to the conclusion (and hence the premises) is that many leaders of totalitarian one-party states *haven't* done anything nearly as bad as what Stalin did. Take a moment to review the post-Stalin list of leaders of the Soviet Union. Not even the conservative Brezhnev, never mind liberalizers like Khrushchev or Gorbachev, committed any abuses even approaching the scale of Stalin's crimes.

Granted, between the hysteria of the Great Purge and the deportation of entire nationalities, Stalin set the bar pretty high. And Khrushchev, for example, sent Soviet tanks into Hungary in 1956 to crush the Hungarians' attempt to experiment with a more humane and democratic version of socialism. (Similarly, although he denies the charges, Gorbachev has been accused of complicity with an attempt at organizing an anti-democratic coup in Lithuania in 1990 to stop the Lithuanians from seceding from the USSR.) If 'Stalin-like outcomes' means any abuse of the same *kind* as what Stalin did, no matter how much milder the scale, perhaps these qualify.

If so, though, 'Stalin-like' deeds are more common for major world leaders than one might have thought. Dwight D. Eisenhower's CIA overthrew the democratically elected left-wing government of Guatemala in 1954, an act that led to a far greater death toll than Khrushchev's quashing of the Hungarian Revolution. The same is true of Ronald Reagan's backing of the Contra death squads that fought to overthrow the democratically elected left-wing government of Nicaragua in the 1980s. Were Eisenhower and Reagan 'Stalin-like' leaders? I'm not interested in promoting whataboutery—nothing about what happened in Guatemala excuses Hungary any more than Soviet crimes in Hungary excuse American imperialism—but in exploring what Peterson is trying to get at, since at the bare minimum he seems to be suggesting that communism is inherently *more evil* than America's combination of corporate capitalism, reasonably democratic two-party elections and an imperial presidency. If this assumption about his views is correct, the bar for 'Stalin-like outcomes' should therefore be set higher than an Eisenhower— or Reagan—level of evil...which again, casts doubt on the conclusion that I suggested follows from his premises (and hence on the premises themselves).

A deeper problem, though, is that his broader implied

conclusion about *Marxism* doesn't follow from any of the premises we've extracted from his video. Perhaps we could charitably interpret what he's saying as an *enthymeme*—an argument where some of the premises are not explicitly stated. But what's missing? Assuming that the conclusion is, 'Any attempt to implement a Marxist political programme would lead to a Stalin-like outcome,' it seems to me that he needs this extra premise:

> **Premise Three**: If a Stalin-like outcome would result from either of these two scenarios, then any attempt to implement a Marxist political programme would lead to a Stalin-like outcome.

Why on *earth*, though, should we believe that?

If Peterson isn't relying on something like Premise Three, then I have no idea why he thinks a broad conclusion about *Marxism* leading to Stalin-like results follows from anything that he's said. If he is, however, then the whole thing relies on at least two nested logical fallacies—a False Dilemma ('attempts to implement a Marxist political programme would mean Stalin being in charge of a Stalinist one-party state or one of his retroactive critics having been in charge of one') premised on what is, if you know anything at all about the history of socialist thought, a hilariously bizarre Strawman ('anti-Stalinist Marxists advocate the creation of a totalitarian one-party state and believe that the problem was that the one that was created in the Soviet Union wasn't led by individuals of sufficient moral integrity'). Marxists very emphatically reject the idea that historical outcomes are a matter of which individuals happen to be in charge of social structures rather than the nature of the structures themselves. When Marxists make a big point of calling themselves 'historical materialists', it's precisely because we're interested in distancing ourselves from *that* conception of history. There's been a long (and in fact *uninterrupted*) tradition of Western (and some non-Western) Marxists criticizing the Soviet model, starting with Rosa Luxemburg's pamphlet *The Russian Revolution* (which was published within months of the revolution, and showed a remarkable amount of foresight on Luxemburg's part about the seeds of Stalinism that had already been planted) and going through people like Leon Trotsky, Max Shachtman, Tony Cliff, Ted Grant, Ernest Mandel, Hal Draper and Michael Harrington among many, many others. These figures criticized the Soviet Communists not for putting morally impure people in charge of their totalitarian one-party state *but for setting up a totalitarian one-party state in the first place.* Instead, their socialist vision was retaining a free press and multi-party elections while expanding democracy to the foundations of the economy through the collective democratic control of factories, farms and other workplaces.

Given that the ultimate target of Peterson's critique is Marxism *per se,* not any particular interpretation of it, an obvious follow-up question is whether the Stalinists or their critics were closer to the views of Marx himself. On that question, for anyone who knows anything about Marx's writings, there's simply no room for serious disagreement. Marx was a critic of censorship and of the death penalty. In his Inaugural Address to the International Workingmen's Association, he praised worker-run cooperatives as anticipatory models of a socialist economy—while he thought the whole economy could only be brought under workers' control by 'national means' (i.e. using political action rather than hoping to outcompete the capitalists in the marketplace), he wrote that 'these great social experiments' proved in practice that 'modern industrial production' is possible without dividing society into 'a class of masters' and 'a class of hands'. (Despite the fact that traditional capitalist businesses have obvious competitive advantages over coops in markets left to their own devices— it's easier to keep wages down to free up funds with which to rapidly expand your business if the people being paid low wages don't get a vote in the matter — a great deal more evidence along these lines has accumulated since Marx's time. While Peterson may think that humans are as biologically predestined toward hierarchical economic arrangements as lobsters, in the real world, the Mondragon Corporation in Spain has grown over the several decades of its existence to 85,000 members and become one of the largest employers in the country.)

Not only did Marx not support any revolutionary dictators in his lifetime, the only head of state he ever thought highly enough of to write the man a friendly telegram on the occasion of his re-election was one Abraham Lincoln, who Marx supported for obvious anti-slavery reasons. He supported violent revolutions against monarchies (and against republics that didn't give working-class people the right to vote) but as the franchise started to be extended to ordinary workers in countries like England, he started to hold out hope that workers in such countries could non-violently vote a socialist government into power. (He did worry that once this happened English factory-owners would respond the way American slave-owners had responded to the election of Lincoln.) While there *were* plenty of nineteenth century socialists who thought a transition to socialism could be achieved through a small elite conspiratorially taking power and acting on behalf of the working class, Marx himself and his close collaborator Engels were — as Hal Draper documents in his classic pamphlet *The Two Souls of Socialism* — fierce critics of such schemes. They talked in a few places of a collective dictatorship of the entire working class ('the dictatorship of the proletariat') but the real-world model they pointed to in order to explain what they meant by this phrase was the ultra-democratic Paris Commune created by rebellious French workers and soldiers in 1871. The features of the Commune praised by Marx in his tract *The Civil War in France* included abandoned factories being turned over to 'associations of workers', the pay of elected officials being kept down to the average wages of skilled workers, and all elected officials being recallable by their constituents at any time and for any reason. That doesn't sound to me like someone whose plan for delivering socialism was putting all power into the hands of a morally pure version of Joseph Stalin.

The problem, of course, is that Peterson doesn't know any of this. He may collect Soviet art and maintain an interest in the psychology of totalitarianism, but his knowledge of Marx's writings is non-existent. At the beginning of his debate with Slavoj Žižek, Peterson mentioned in passing that, before re-reading *The Communist Manifesto* in preparation for his debate with one of the world's most famous Marxist intellectuals, he hadn't read it since he was 18 years old. For a middle-aged man who's spent years ranting and raving about the evils of 'Marxism' at every opportunity, that's an absolutely stunning admission. As my friend Michael Brooks dryly puts it in his book *Against the Web,* 'If he hadn't felt moved to pick up Marx's shortest and most popular book at any point in the last few decades…it's safe to say Peterson hasn't been poring over the three volumes of *Capital*.' Moreover—see Conrad Hamilton's discussion of this point in Chapter Nine, or Benjamin Studebaker's *Current Affairs* article 'How Žižek Should Have Replied to Jordan Peterson'—it's hard to believe that the good professor gave even the *Manifesto* more than a light skim.

This brings us to another problem with Peterson's argumentative and rhetorical style. As pretty much everyone to have written about him has noted, Peterson likes to present himself as a sort of stern intellectual father figure—as the girls on the *Red Scare* podcast might put it, he's 'lobster daddy'. He's most comfortable either explicating his findings to a rapt audience or dressing down his opponents for their moral fecklessness. Either way, the implied argument often seems to be:

Premise One: Jordan Peterson is a very smart guy who's spent a lot of time looking into this stuff.

Premise Two: Jordan Peterson's considered conclusion is X.

Conclusion: X is probably true.

This sort of argument does have its place. Given that we can't all be experts in every field, we do often need an epistemic division of labour whereby some become experts in one thing, others become experts in another, and we report our findings back to each other. The difference between the Appeal to Authority logical fallacy and a legitimate appeal to expert opinion is whether the figure being appealed to really does have expertise lacked by the rest of us.

Peterson is an expert in Jungian psychoanalysis. (Since my own academic background is in logic-chopping analytic philosophy, I'm strongly tempted to view Jungian psychoanalysis as bullshit, but I'll assume for the sake of argument that this is unfair.) When it comes to the history of socialist thought, though, he *acts* like an expert—that is to say, he constantly makes assertions without bothering to cite texts or any other support beyond his own implied deep store of knowledge—but he's a complete ignoramus. Similarly with the law. As Matt McManus points out in Chapter One, Peterson rose to prominence on the basis of *extremely* dubious claims about the implications of a civil rights law in which the word 'pronoun' does not appear. (Its primary purpose is to protect trans people against employment discrimination, housing discrimination and other matters weightier than having a psychology prof without the basic good manners to call you by your preferred pronouns.) In fact, the actual experts on that one—the Canadian Bar Association—put out a statement decisively rejecting the claim that C-16 would 'force individuals to embrace concepts, or even use pronouns, which they find objectionable'. (Sadly, Professor Lobster Daddy has a far larger popular audience than the Canadian

Bar Association, especially on the US side of the border.) Most bizarrely, in an August 2018 interview with the BBC's Stephen Sackur, Peterson literally says the words, 'I am an evolutionary biologist.' For a psychologist with no special training of any kind in biology, claims to unearned authority don't get much more brazen than that. But he *seems* authoritative, so his fans— and all too many fence-sitting casual observers--don't register the oddness of these claims.

When someone projects the image of a stern patriarch, so morally upright that he's often emotionally overcome by indignation at the wickedness of his enemies and so knowledgeable on so many subjects that he felt comfortable quoting Matthew 13:35 as the epigraph of *Maps of Meaning* ('I will utter things that have been kept secret since the foundation of the world'), your instinct—to the extent that you take this image at face value—will be to mull over his odder pronouncements instead of coming right out and demanding to know what he means. This too is deeply dangerous.

Let's consider, one last time, the 'enforced monogamy' brouhaha. Peterson was quoted in the *New York Times* as saying that the 'cure' for violence against women committed by self-described 'incels' was 'enforced monogamy'. In various statements, including a written one on his website ('On the New York Times and "Enforced Monogamy"'), he waxes indignant and aggrieved about how his 'motivated critics' have interpreted this as a sinister and misogynistic proposal. He angrily denies any suggestion that he supports 'police-state assignation of women to men (or men to women)' or dealing out 'damsels to incels' or anything else 'scandalous'. Rather, he's just supporting 'socially enforced monogamous conventions' —i.e. society having a taboo against non-monogamous practices.

What could be 'scandalous' about that? After all, the society we live in pretty clearly *does* have a wide variety of social conventions rewarding monogamous pairing and discouraging deviations from it. (It would be a very unusual high school, for example, that would reward a boy who brought two girls to the prom by naming them Prom King and Co-Queens.) At this point, it's an accepted article of faith in lobster world that anyone who brings up 'enforced monogamy' in the course of critiquing Peterson is being unfair if not outright libellous.

But wait. Thirty seconds of consideration should show that Peterson's 'explanation' actually explains nothing. We already have various social conventions favouring monogamy. We also have incel killers. So if Peterson wants to argue that the *solution* to the latter is enforcement of monogamy, the only way this even adds up to a coherent thought is if he's suggesting that we should be doing *more* than we already are to enforce monogamy. Well—*what* more, specifically? He doesn't say—probably because just about any *specific* proposal for how society could do *more* to discourage promiscuity, infidelity, polyamory and other deviations from monogamous norms would almost certainly be controversial enough to strike some portion of the audience he was trying to reassure as...well...'scandalous'.

Peterson's move here is a version of the Fallacy of Equivocation (the way that an argument can go wrong when a key term is used to mean different things at different points in a reasoning process) called the 'Motte and Bailey' strategy. This is an analogy to medieval warfare used by British philosophy professor Nicholas Schackel in his paper 'The Vacuity of Postmodernist Methodology'.

A Motte and Bailey castle is a medieval system of defence in which a stone tower on a mound (the Motte) is surrounded by an area of land (the Bailey) which in turn is encompassed by some sort of a barrier such as a ditch. Being dark and dank, the Motte is not a habitation of choice. The only reason for its existence is the desirability of the Bailey, which the combination of the Motte and ditch makes relatively easy to retain despite attack by marauders. When only lightly pressed, the ditch makes small numbers of attackers easy to defeat as they struggle across it: when heavily pressed the ditch is not defensible and so neither is the Bailey. Rather one retreats to the insalubrious but defensible, perhaps impregnable, Motte. Eventually the marauders give up, when one is well placed to reoccupy desirable land.

For my purposes the desirable but only lightly defensible territory of the Motte and Bailey castle, that is to say, the Bailey, represents a philosophical doctrine or position with similar properties: desirable to its proponent but only lightly defensible. The Motte is the defensible but undesired position to which one retreats when hard pressed.

You've almost certainly heard firebrand conservative politicians use this strategy. You know how it goes. First, a clearly inflammatory and racist claim about immigrants is thrown out as red meat for the politician's base. Then, after the critics have savaged the politician for the original statement, he trots out a reinterpretation about crime and social services so carefully worded as to be hard to dispute. 'All I was saying was...'

In Peterson's case I frankly suspect that things might be even worse than that. My co-authors have laboured mightily to charitably interpret Peterson's many odd pronouncements before critiquing him, and I thank them for their service, but I also worry that when it comes to figures like Peterson interpretive charity can all too easily be stretched beyond its useful limits. He may be a very smart man, genuinely knowledgeable and curious about at least some of the subjects on which he pronounces, but he's also a man who's spent his public life trading on the persuasive power of his electrifying preacher-like rhetoric. It might be all too easy for someone like that to throw out a vague statement—knowing that his loyal lobsters will like the sound of it, and that the feminists and leftists he so reviles will *hate* it—without meaning much of *anything* in particular. The Motte, in his case, may just be a vague conceptual smudge in the middle of the Bailey, the spot where a worked-out thought might go if he had one to offer.

Perhaps I'm being unfair. Peterson himself makes a constant practice of attributing unsavoury motivations to his ideological enemies—socialists don't *really* care about the poor, they *really* just resent their more dominant and successful fellow-lobsters—but perhaps I should be setting a higher standard here and refraining from speculating about what's going on in the good professor's head. Perhaps. One way or the other, though, if Peterson wants to complain about being misrepresented, he owes us clearer explanations of what he *did* mean to say. And if he wants to be taken seriously on subjects like socialism and feminism and monogamy and evolution and civil rights law by those *not* spellbound by his rhetoric, he should give us better arguments.

Endnotes

1. Thagard, Paul. 'Jordan Peterson's Murky Maps of Meaning,' *Psychology Today*. 12 March 2018.
2. From the video 'Jordan Peterson—The Lion King Part 1,' available on YouTube.
3. Given that Peterson tends to utilize his extensive readings on the subject of totalitarianism as a cudgel to bludgeon the Left and/or civil rights causes with—and is comparatively coy in admonishing the Right, who perhaps not coincidentally make up a greater share of his avid online following—Doidge's valorization of Peterson as an avowed opponent of reaction is, of course, overstated (one wonders, for instance, what Doidge would think of Peterson's May 2019 meeting with Viktor Orban, a politician who's presented himself as the saviour of Hungary from Jewish financiers and who's sought to rehabilitate Hungarians complicit in the Holocaust). Though it is true that in his books, Peterson frequently cites impassionedly, and indulgently, from texts describing the horrors of totalitarianism, to the point where by the end of the fifth chapter of *Maps of Meaning* you just about expect him to start liberally quoting from *The Diary of Anne Frank*. To understand this contradiction, it helps to understand the particular culture of Canada, in which a kind of faux-benevolent liberalism is used to ensure the continuity of the governance of the country by 50 or so corporations. When I went to a public school in Ontario in the '90s and 2000s, for instance, the non-Shakespeare required reading list went something like this (I approximate): *The Giver, The Chrysalids, The Lord of the Flies, 1984, Animal Farm*. Many of these, of course, are substantial pieces of literature. But taken collectively, their selection betrays, over and above any particular concern for the plight of ethnic minorities, a

pathological obsession with the notion of *totalitarianism*, or the risks posed to bourgeois order and basic decency by the spectre of mass rule. That such a culture, when exposed to the volatility of post-2007-08, could produce an individual like Peterson—whose avowed disdain of authoritarianism seems to function as a cover for the composition of his audience, not to mention the content of his statements—is, therefore, not surprising.

4. Perhaps the nadir of Peterson's near-residence at *The Agenda* comes during a 4-minute segment of 'Agenda Insight' in 2011 titled 'Goodbye to Good Men'—guess, just guess— in which Peterson claims that the society-wide effort to repress 'masculine impulses' (his son being prohibited from throwing snowballs at school, for instance) is causing men to withdraw from socioromantic engagement. In Peterson's view—one uncomfortably similar to that espoused by many pick-up artists and/or men's rights activists—this threatens to create a situation in which 'aggressive, psychopathic men' increasingly enjoy a monopoly on sexual partners ('that'll keep the testosterone flowing').

5. In Peterson's words: 'He had Mia, the book's female lead, post a selection of them, one by one, on her fridge, at points in the story where they seemed apropos.'

6. *The National Post*'s original parent company, Black's Hollinger Inc., founded the paper in 1998 partly with the objective of challenging the political domination of the Liberal Party after the spectacular collapse of the Tories in the 1993 Canadian federal election—which at first meant giving a great deal of support to Stockwell Day, the leader of the residually Alberta-centric Canadian Alliance (to give you an idea of Day's character, when asked why 'his party did not offer condolences to the Palestinians when Yasser Arafat died Stock responded by sending out a column by David Frum that speculated that Yasser died of AIDS'). Hollinger

Inc. eventually went bankrupt in 2007 amidst the scandal that led to Black's imprisonment, selling its Canadian assets to Canwest, who in turn went into bankruptcy protection in 2009 and sold its newspaper arm to Postmedia. Cataclysmic end or no, Hollinger Inc. did manage to significantly change the Canadian news media culture, enforcing corporate editorial positions with an iron fist and hollowing out much of progressive news space so that it could be filled with e.g. adverts paid for by oil-and-gas disguised as articles (Postmedia's 'sponsored energy content' policy).

7. Full disclosure: I have a soft spot for Black because, after I wrote him an email during his years of imprisonment criticizing an article on Lovelock's Gaia hypothesis, he wrote back. Full response: 'I call 'em as I see 'em.' More seriously, while it's been unfortunate seeing him cheerlead for Trump in recent years, Black's biography of FDR, 2003's *Franklin Delano Roosevelt: Champion of Freedom*, represents a major effort by a conservative thinker to dislodge, or at least to tame, the neoclassical economic consensus (in this case, the revisionist idea, advocated by Milton Friedman and others, that the New Deal *worsened* the Great Depression). And this was years before the 2007-08 crisis.

8. The Ottawa Public Library choosing to host Peterson is yet another example of the willingness of public institutions in Canada to accommodate the far right. Nor is it the only instance of this sort of accommodation to have occurred in the capital region: in December 2016, after a screening of Cassie Jaye's pro-MRA documentary *The Red Pill* at the Mayfair Theatre was cancelled due to complaints, Ottawa City Hall surreally agreed to host the event. Like Faith Goldy or Peterson protégé Lindsey Sheperd, a 'cute girl-next-door' who is, crucially, white, Jaye—with her stated intention to take a 'balanced approach' to MRAs—is herself a good case study in the kind of banality that can lead to the promotion

of fascist ideas.

9. Another Twitter ponderable from Peterson, this one from 3 March 2017: '91% of those who view my videos are male. Why? Why so few women?'

10. During his response to the question on race and IQ at Lafayette College, Peterson alludes to having given thought to the subject due to having been asked about 'the Jewish question' by 'someone Jewish' at one of his talks. This question, he claims, was subsequently taken out of context by *Vice*, who used it 'as an indication of the quality of people who are my so-called followers'. In reality, Peterson wants you to know that the quality of those who regularly watch his videos on YouTube is 'pretty darn high', as a cursory overview of their comments, 'head and shoulders above the standard set', demonstrates. The incident in question appears to have occurred at the Kaye Playhouse in New York City on 23 January 2018—the same date *12 Rules for Life* was published in Canada. During the talk, a self-described 'Jewish American' audience member asks Peterson a pre-prepared question about whether Solzhenitsyn's assertion in *Two Hundred Years Together*—that the 'ethnic hatred' felt by the disproportionately Jewish 'NKVD and Bolshevik leaders' towards Christians influenced their actions in the Holodomor—could be read into the current tensions with Russia. Jews, he reasons, are 'overrepresented' in the 'US news media'—an agglomerate that is also 'inexplicably hostile' towards 'Russia' and 'Russian Christians'. Peterson, after placing his head in his hands and pacing to the edge of the stage and back—a signature gesture meant to imply a deep state of contemplation—begins to ponder aloud whether he can formulate a response: 'It's so difficult to disentangle.' Then, as jeers continue to rain down upon his inquisitor, he finally capitulates: 'I can't do it.' The three first comments that appear, in aggregate, on the video excerpt

of Peterson's response to this question, are, as of 9 August 2018, by the way: 1) 'That's the 6 million dollar question', 2) 'oy vey, shut it down' and 3) 'All the kvetching at his question. The mere fact that questions like these are starting to be asked is promising though. Five years ago the mic feed would have been cut midway through.'

11. This propensity was parodied in a highly astute holiday-themed meme that made the rounds in February 2019, which portrays Peterson advising 'feminists + postmodern leftists' who claim Valentine's Day is a social construct to 'go to a calendar' and 'look'.

12. The term 'unconscious' [*Unbewusste*] was actually coined by Friedrich Schelling in his 1800 *System of Transcendental Idealism*; he argued in the text that consciousness is subordinated to the unconscious in artistic creation—an idea that predicts the work of Freud, who would later refer to artists as 'master sublimizers'.

13. On 7 June 2018, Kathleen Wynne's Liberal government fell, and was replaced by the Progressive Conservative government of Doug Ford—the brother of late Toronto mayor Rob Ford, a proto-Trump right-wing populist who made international headlines in 2013 due to a video surfacing in *The Toronto Star* of him smoking crack cocaine ('probably in one of my drunken stupors'). After Jordan Peterson publicly urged the Ford Ontario government to 'abolish' the Ontario Human Rights Commission over Twitter on 10 October 2018, Peterson and Ford met one-on-one 8 days later, on 18 October 2018, to 'discuss free speech on Ontario's university and college campuses'. While this meeting was initially not publicized due to the fact that neither party announced it—as well as the fact that Ford does not provide the media with his daily public itinerary, as previous Ontario premiers have—the CBC (Canadian Broadcasting Corporation) drew attention to it in early 2019

after filing a freedom of information request.

14. Jordan Peterson, 'The Unconscious Mind of The SJW,' available on YouTube.

15. As Julia Lovell has observed in her 2019 article in *The Guardian*, 'Maoism marches on: the revolutionary idea that still shapes the world.'

16. This term is not completely off base, at least by far-right standards. While thinkers like Lenin tended to view influencing the domain of culture as ancillary, for the communist movement, to the achievement of political objectives, for Gramsci, the failure of communism to take hold in the most developed countries owed to the 'cultural hegemony' of bourgeois thought. It would thus be necessary, he theorized, for communists to perpetuate their own values and norms, to develop and disseminate their *own* culture, before victory in said countries would be possible (the efforts of Horkheimer and the Frankfurt School to shift institutional/academic cultures are also frequently invoked in reactionary polemics). If the term is semantically correct, though, the alt-right still runs awry of reality in the way they deploy it—namely, to refer to the promulgation of even the most trite identitarian expressions (say, Tumblr users who've chosen to spend their time impassionedly combatting the social panacea of body-shaming). This could nevertheless have an upside. As Steven Shaviro—a thinker whose writings on Whitehead and Speculative Realism easily suffice to make him one of the foremost English-language theoretical voices of our time—has written on Facebook: 'The right-wing blogosphere/twitterverse has increasingly used the phrase "cultural Marxism" to refer to anything having to do with women's rights, gay/lesbian/trans/etc rights, and rights of people of color. They apply this epithet to everything they dislike, even to movies like the most recent Mad Max and Star Wars entries, simply for

having protagonists that are not cis-het white dudes...I for one welcome "cultural Marxism" (thus defined) alongside economic Marxism. Our enemies have made it clear that these are just different aspects of the same struggle.'

17. Much of the description of *La vie la mort* offered here is culled from Francesco Vitale's 2019 essay 'Microphysics of Sex: Sexual Differences between Biology and Deconstruction.'

18. This interview can be found in the 1987 collection of Derrida's interviews and essays pertaining to his political and ethical thinking, *Negotiations: Interventions and Interviews, 1971-2001.*

19. There is no textual source for this, as it was said by Stiegler during the 2016 seminar he gave in Paris as part of the Kent Summer School in Critical Theory, *From German ideology to the Dialectic of nature: Reading Marx and Engels in the age of the Anthropocene.*

20. These remarks are partly derived from Justin Lee's superlative 2018 article 'The Noble Lobster: What Jordan Peterson Understands, and Pankaj Mishra Ignores' [https://www.abc.net.au/religion/the-noble-lobster-what-jordan-peterson-understands-and-pankaj-mi/10094818]

21. On 31 July 1987, President Ronald Reagan nominated Judge Robert Bork for Associate Justice to the Supreme Court of the United States, after the retirement of previous Nixon nominee Lewis Powell. His nomination was blocked, however, by the Democratic Party-controlled Senate, who voiced concerns about the relationship between Bork's constitutional originalism and his attitude towards civil and women's rights, as well as the role he played in helping Nixon depose special prosecutor Richard Cox during the Watergate scandal.

22. Peterson originally sought to organize a series of debates in different cities, but this offer was rejected by Žižek.

23. Žižek's decision to donate to the First Nations Child and

Family Caring Society proved mildly controversial amongst his online fan base, given his past critique of charity as a means of buying 'redemption' from one's own participation in the capitalist economy—precisely what Žižek appeared to be doing.

24. Parts of this account are borrowed from Hal Draper's 1987 text *The 'Dictatorship of the Proletariat' from Marx to Lenin*.

25. We leave to the side here, in this brief explication, the question of the role that the tendency of the profit to fall plays in beckoning the end of capitalism.

26. According to the *Oxfam World Equality Report 2018*, co-authored by Thomas Piketty.

zer0
books

CULTURE, SOCIETY & POLITICS

The modern world is at an impasse. Disasters scroll across our
smartphone screens and we're invited to like, follow or upvote, but
critical thinking is harder and harder to find. Rather than connect-
ing us in common struggle and debate, the internet has sped up
and deepened a long-standing process of alienation and atomiza-
tion. Zer0 Books wants to work against this trend.
With critical theory as our jumping off point, we aim to publish
books that make our readers uncomfortable. We want to move
beyond received opinions.
Zer0 Books is on the left and wants to reinvent the left. We are sick
of the injustice, the suffering, and the stupidity that defines both
our political and cultural world, and we aim to find a new foundation for a new struggle.

If this book has helped you to clarify an idea, solve a problem or
extend your knowledge, you may want to check out our online
content as well. Look for Zer0 Books: Advancing Conversations in
the iTunes directory and for our Zer0 Books YouTube channel.

Popular videos include:

Žižek and the Double Blackmain

The Intellectual Dark Web is a Bad Sign

Can there be an Anti-SJW Left?

Answering Jordan Peterson on Marxism

Follow us on Facebook
at https://www.facebook.com/ZeroBooks and Twitter at
https://twitter.com/Zer0Books

Bestsellers from Zer0 Books include:

Give Them An Argument
Logic for the Left
Ben Burgis
Many serious leftists have learned to distrust talk of logic. This is a
serious mistake.
Paperback: 978-1-78904-210-8 ebook: 978-1-78904-211-5

Poor but Sexy
Culture Clashes in Europe East and West
Agata Pyzik
How the East stayed East and the West stayed West.
Paperback: 978-1-78099-394-2 ebook: 978-1-78099-395-9

An Anthropology of Nothing in Particular
Martin Demant Frederiksen
A journey into the social lives of meaninglessness.
Paperback: 978-1-78535-699-5 ebook: 978-1-78535-700-8

In the Dust of This Planet
Horror of Philosophy vol. 1
Eugene Thacker
In the first of a series of three books on the Horror of Philosophy,
In the Dust of This Planet offers the genre of horror as a way of
thinking about the unthinkable.
Paperback: 978-1-84694-676-9 ebook: 978-1-78099-010-1

The End of Oulipo?
An Attempt to Exhaust a Movement
Lauren Elkin, Veronica Esposito
Paperback: 978-1-78099-655-4 ebook: 978-1-78099-656-1

Capitalist Realism
Is There no Alternative?
Mark Fisher
An analysis of the ways in which capitalism has presented itself as
the only realistic political-economic system.
Paperback: 978-1-84694-317-1 ebook: 978-1-78099-734-6

Rebel Rebel
Chris O'Leary
David Bowie: every single song. Everything you want to know,
everything you didn't know.
Paperback: 978-1-78099-244-0 ebook: 978-1-78099-713-1

Kill All Normies
Angela Nagle
Online culture wars from 4chan and Tumblr to Trump.
Paperback: 978-1- 78535-543-1 ebook: 978-1-78535-544-8

Cartographies of the Absolute
Alberto Toscano, Jeff Kinkle
An aesthetics of the economy for the twenty-first century.
Paperback: 978-1-78099-275-4 ebook: 978-1-78279-973-3

Malign Velocities
Accelerationism and Capitalism
Benjamin Noys
Long listed for the Bread and Roses Prize 2015, *Malign Velocities*
argues against the need for speed, tracking acceleration
as the symptom of the ongoing crises of capitalism.
Paperback: 978-1-78279-300-7 ebook: 978-1-78279-299-4

Meat Market
Female Flesh under Capitalism
Laurie Penny
A feminist dissection of women's bodies as the fleshy fulcrum of
capitalist cannibalism, whereby women are both consumers and
consumed.
Paperback: 978-1-84694-521-2 ebook: 978-1-84694-782-7

Babbling Corpse
Vaporwave and the Commodification of Ghosts
Grafton Tanner
Paperback: 978-1-78279-759-3 ebook: 978-1-78279-760-9

New Work New Culture
Work we want and a culture that strengthens us
Frithjoff Bergmann
A serious alternative for mankind and the planet.
Paperback: 978-1-78904-064-7 ebook: 978-1-78904-065-4

Romeo and Juliet in Palestine
Teaching Under Occupation
Tom Sperlinger
Life in the West Bank, the nature of pedagogy and the role of a
university under occupation.
Paperback: 978-1-78279-637-4 ebook: 978-1-78279-636-7

Ghosts of My Life
Writings on Depression, Hauntology and Lost Futures
Mark Fisher
Paperback: 978-1-78099-226-6 ebook: 978-1-78279-624-4

Sweetening the Pill
or How We Got Hooked on Hormonal Birth Control
Holly Grigg-Spall
Has contraception liberated or oppressed women?
Sweetening the Pill breaks the silence on the dark side of hormonal
contraception.
Paperback: 978-1-78099-607-3 ebook: 978-1-78099-608-0

Why Are We The Good Guys?
Reclaiming your Mind from the Delusions of Propaganda
David Cromwell
A provocative challenge to the standard ideology that Western
power is a benevolent force in the world.
Paperback: 978-1-78099-365-2 ebook: 978-1-78099-366-9

The Writing on the Wall
On the Decomposition of Capitalism and its Critics
Anselm Jappe, Alastair Hemmens
A new approach to the meaning of social emancipation.
Paperback: 978-1-78535-581-3 ebook: 978-1-78535-582-0

Enjoying It
Candy Crush and Capitalism
Alfie Bown
A study of enjoyment and of the enjoyment of studying. Bown asks
what enjoyment says about us and what we say about enjoyment,
and why.
Paperback: 978-1-78535-155-6 ebook: 978-1-78535-156-3

Color, Facture, Art and Design
Iona Singh
This materialist definition of fine-art develops guidelines for
architecture, design, cultural-studies and ultimately social change.
Paperback: 978-1-78099-629-5 ebook: 978-1-78099-630-1

Neglected or Misunderstood
The Radical Feminism of Shulamith Firestone
Victoria Margree
An interrogation of issues surrounding gender, biology, sexual-
ity, work and technology, and the ways in which our imaginations
continue to be in thrall to ideologies of maternity and the nuclear
family.
Paperback: 978-1-78535-539-4 ebook: 978-1-78535-540-0

How to Dismantle the NHS in 10 Easy Steps (Second Edition)
Youssef El-Gingihy
The story of how your NHS was sold off and why you will have to
buy private health insurance soon. A new expanded second edition
with chapters on junior doctors' strikes and government blueprints
for US-style healthcare.
Paperback: 978-1-78904-178-1 ebook: 978-1-78904-179-8

Digesting Recipes
The Art of Culinary Notation
Susannah Worth
A recipe is an instruction, the imperative tone of the expert, but
this constraint can offer its own kind of potential. A recipe need
not be a domestic trap but might instead offer escape – something
to fantasise about or aspire to.

Paperback: 978-1-78279-860-6 ebook: 978-1-78279-859-0

Most titles are published in paperback and as an ebook.
Paperbacks are available in traditional bookshops. Both print and
ebook formats are available online.
Follow us on Facebook
at https://www.facebook.com/ZeroBooks
and Twitter at https://twitter.com/Zer0Books